COMPUTER
NETWORKING FOR
BEGINNERS

Your Guide For Mastering Computer Networking,
Cisco IOS And The OSI Model

TABLE OF CONTENTS

Introduction

First of all, I want to congratulate and thank you for deciding to invest in yourself and become better.

After you finish this eBook, you'll be able to understand:

- How the Internet works
- How end-devices (such as smartphones, laptops, tablets) communicate on the Internet
- How do our networks work and how many types of networks there are
- What is a Router, a Switch, an IP address, or a MAC Address
- How can we apply this knowledge to practical scenarios
- How does the Routing and Switching process work
- Why do we need static routes or routing protocols
- What's the purpose of a VLAN in a network

This book is structured into **13 significant chapters** that will cover various topics belonging to the computer networking world.

What to expect from this book?

This Computer Networking book will teach you all the basic stuff you need to know about Networking and how the Internet works. The first seven chapters are more theoretical and will cover the communication process of devices (PCs, laptops, smartphones, tablets, etc.) within a network.

The first part of the book will be geared toward understanding the **OSI model**, which is a framework that defines the way devices communicate with the Internet (and in our LANs). The OSI model is divided into **seven layers**, each with a crucial part in communication. We'll spend our time learning about network cables, MAC and IP addresses, TCP and UDP ports, and network applications (such as HTTPS, SSH, DNS, etc.)

From **chapter 8 to chapter 13,** you will be introduced to the practical world of computer networking with real-life scenarios that you can create and practice on your laptop or desktop with the help of the Cisco Packet Tracer simulator. We'll be focusing on configuring Cisco network devices. **Cisco** is the leading vendor in the networking space (similar to what Apple does in the smartphone area), and its widespread being the reason for our choice of using it. These network devices are configured through a terminal from a CLI (Command Line Interface) and the commands that will be used will be listed according to the chapters (with the topic to be applied) of the book.

Thank you and happy reading!

Ramon Nastase

PS: As a Gift, I want to give, for FREE, access to my six steps guide on starting (and performing) as an IT Specialist in today's digital world. Claim your FREE guide by accessing this page: **https://bit.ly/IT-GIFT,** or you can scan the QR code:

You can also check out one of my other books on Amazon.com by clicking this link: https://amzn.to/2zE72Wm

Chapter 1

Basic Networking Elements

A the **network** is a group of **interconnected** devices (PCs, Laptops, Servers, smartphones, etc.) that can communicate (exchange information) with each other. These devices communicate through special network equipment (**Routers** and **Switches**). We'll talk more about Routers and Switches in later chapters. For now, let's see the existing network types.

1) Network Types

Computer networks can be:

- **LAN** – *Local Area Network* – your home network
- **MAN** – *Metropolitan Area Network* – extended network covering the entire surface of a city
- **WAN** – *Wide Area Network* – multiple networks (LANs) of an organization, which are interconnected
- **WWAN** – *World Wide Area Network* – the Internet

- **WLAN** – *Wireless LAN* – aka Wi-Fi, which is usually created by our home Router

In addition to these network types, there are others of different sizes or purposes (e.g., SAN - Storage Area Network, EPN – Enterprise Private Network, VPN – Virtual Private Network).

Now let's take a closer look at some of the networks mentioned above:

A **LAN** is a relatively small network that is **local to an organization** or a home. For example, your home network is considered a LAN because it limits the number of devices.

A school network (although larger than a home network) is considered a LAN because it interconnects many devices (all computers, servers, etc.) in the same network.

Moving forward to the next network type: if we were to combine multiple networks and allow them to interconnect within a city, then we would form a **MAN** (a much wider network, which would be spread across an entire city. This type of network offers *higher transfer speeds* of data than the usual Internet connection).

As I said earlier, a MAN is a network that interconnects multiple networks within a city. The purpose of a **WAN** is to connect the network of multiple cities (or even countries) to form a wider network across a large geographical area. We can also say that *numerous LANs* of an organization (or numerous organizations) that are interconnected form a WAN.

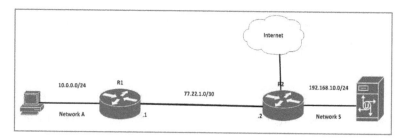

Figure 1.1

For example, in figure 1.1, you can see 2 Routers, 1 PC and 1 Server. The connection between the PC and Router R1 forms a LAN (the same for R2 and the Server). The connection between the 2 Routers will form a WAN because they are connecting multiple networks. If you're confused, don't worry! We'll talk about all of these concepts in depth throughout this book.

A **WLAN** (aka Wi-Fi) is a LAN to which we can connect wireless from our smartphones, tablets, laptops, or any other device. The wireless environment is separate from the physical (cable) one and has different properties in terms of speed, security, coverage, etc. The main benefit of Wireless connectivity is the flexibility that it offers.

2) Network Topologies

In a typical network environment, there can be multiple representations of devices. These devices can be grouped in various ways, considering what different purposes they are serving.

For example, if we only care for network connectivity (or Internet access), we'll group the devices in a **star-like topology**. The problem in this scenario would be the lack of redundancy (a very important part of computer networking).

So, if we intend to have a very reliable network (such as one of an ISP - Internet Service Provider), then we would use a **mesh topology**. Let's take a closer look at the different types of network representations in the figures below:

In figure 1.2, we have the **Star Topology** that we spoke of earlier. The interconnected devices are Switches (network devices that connect us to a LAN – and we're going to talk about these in depth a little bit later). Here's a visual representation of what a network would look like:

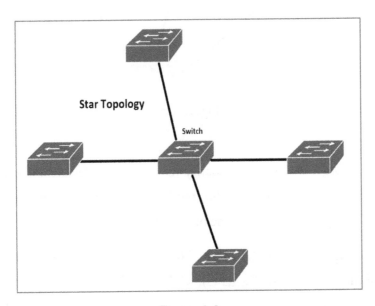

Figure 1.2

Next in our topology design, we have our Switches connected in a **Full Mesh Topology** (figure 1.3). This topology allows for full redundancy. If something bad happens with a cable or a Switch, there will be redundant ways to reach the Internet or a different destination.

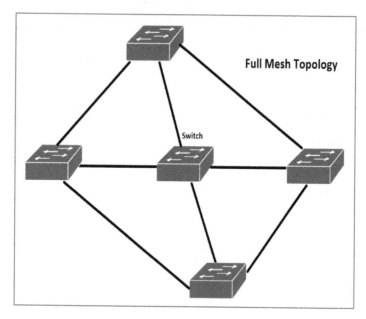

Figure 1.3

Let's not forget that full redundancy requires more devices and cabling (which implies more money). So, the full mesh topology will be more expensive to implement than the one in figure 1.4

The 3rd topology is **Partial Mesh**. This provides redundancy only for a part of the network (and Switches), while the other Switches are left with a "single way out". This topology is a cheaper version than the Full Mesh implementation.

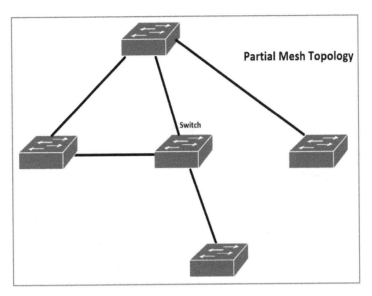

Figure 1.4

And last but not least is the Hub and Spoke. This one is very often used in the WAN (Internet) design. The 3 Routers in this topology don't know each other by default, so both R1 and R3 will have to send their data (aka. traffic) to R2, which knows how to redirect the traffic to reach its destination.

For example, if R1 wants to send traffic to R3, they will send it to the Hub (R2), as it knows what to do with it (where to redirect it). This design is being used because it scales. We only have 3 Routers in this representation, but what will you do when you have 20, 80, and 200? Then it will be challenging to track all of them (or assign paths manually to certain destinations).

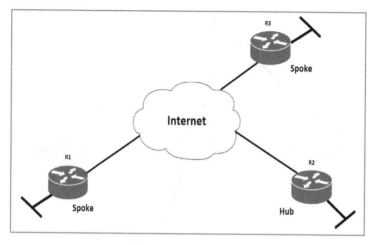

Figure 1.5

3) Network Components

Now let's move forward and speak a bit about the components that form a network:

- **End-device** - (PC, Laptop, smartphone, Servers, etc.)
- **Switch** - interconnects multiple end-devices within a network (LAN)
- **Router** - interconnects multiple networks (thus, forming a WAN)
- **Firewall** - protects our network from potential cyber-attacks
- **Transmission medium** – the way information is transmitted (e.g., through cable or wireless)

Let's take a closer look at the network components listed above:

A. END DEVICES & MEANS FOR TRANSMISSION

Generally, we are the ones that have a device (end-device). Each of us has a Laptop, tablet, or smartphone with which we connect to the Internet. The connection can be made with one or more transmission media means (electricity, light impulses, radio waves).

When we connect with our smartphones to the Internet, we use the wireless connection. If we are on a Laptop or a PC, we can connect it either wireless or through a network cable (UTP).

Figure 1.6

We use optical fiber when we want to connect multiple networks or server equipment (ex. switch - switch, server - switch). The reason is simple: an optical fiber connection is much faster than UTP (cable) or Wireless. We can transfer more data (10, 40, 100 Gbps throughput) on a longer range (1 - 5 km or miles).

Also, optical fiber is being used when connecting a home user to the Internet. The main reason is that optical fiber can transfer data at higher speeds and at a longer distance (1 - 5 miles/km), which is way better than the classic UTP cable that caps out at 100 meters!

B. SWITCH

A **Switch** (figure 1.7) is a **network device** that *interconnects* multiple end-devices (PCs, laptops, printers, IP phones, Servers, etc.) in the same Local Area Network (*LAN*).

It is well known for its **high port density** (generally **24**, **48**, or even more), capable of speeds between 1 Gbps and 10 Gbps (or even 40 Gbps) per port. The switch uses MAC addresses to identify the end devices connected to the network (we will talk about this in more detail in Chapter 4). Here is an image with a Cisco **Switch**:

Figure 1.7

C. ROUTER

A **Router** is a network device that has the role of **multiple interconnecting networks** (LANs) and forming a larger network (**WAN** - Wide Area

Network). The Router is the (main) device that **connects us to the Internet** through its ability to handle packet delivery from any source (network) to any destination (network).

The Router achieves this by using **IP addresses** to identify the source and the destination devices (we'll talk more about IP addresses in Chapter 3).

When comparing it to a Switch, the Router has way fewer ports (between 2 to 5) at similar speeds (100 Mbps - 10Gbps, depending on the model). Bellow, you can see a Cisco **Router**:

Figure 1.8

4) How can we represent (or "draw") a network?

Usually, networks are **represented** by a "**network topology**", which can be of 2 types: **logical** or **physical**. Logical topologies describe the logical aspects of a network: the IP addresses of the networks, the way the devices are connected, the routing protocols that are being used, etc. The following example is a logical topology composed of 2 Routers, 1 PC, and 1 Server. One of the Routers is connected to the Internet:

Example # 1 Logical Topology

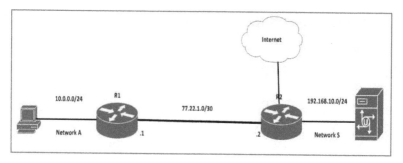

Figure 1.9

In this second example, the network is composed of 1 Switch, 3 Routers, 2 PCs and 1 Server

Example #2 Logical Topology

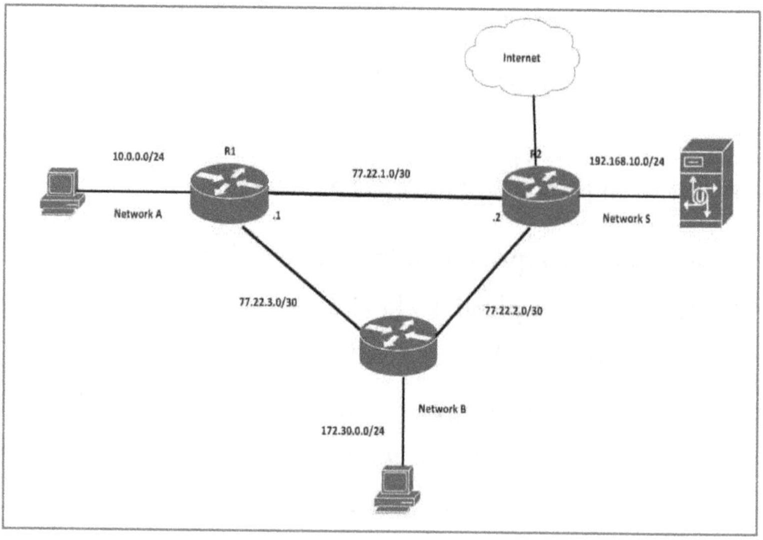

Figure 1.10

Physical topology describes the physical aspect: where the devices are placed, what type of cables we are using, how many ports we need, on what ports/switches will be the servers connected, etc. It shows where the equipment is (physically) located and its main purpose within the network.

5) How do computers communicate over the Internet?

To communicate (send traffic – aka. connect to Facebook, Google, etc.), the devices (PCs, Routers, Switches, etc.) must have a **unique identifier**. This identifier is known as **IP** (**Internet Protocol**) in the Internet world.

The IP is how we identify a device in a network or on the Internet. **It must be unique**. There can't be two equal IP addresses in the same network (or on the Internet) because there will be a conflict and the Internet connection will not work properly. Here are two examples of IP addresses: 192.168.1.170 or 84.222.0.93

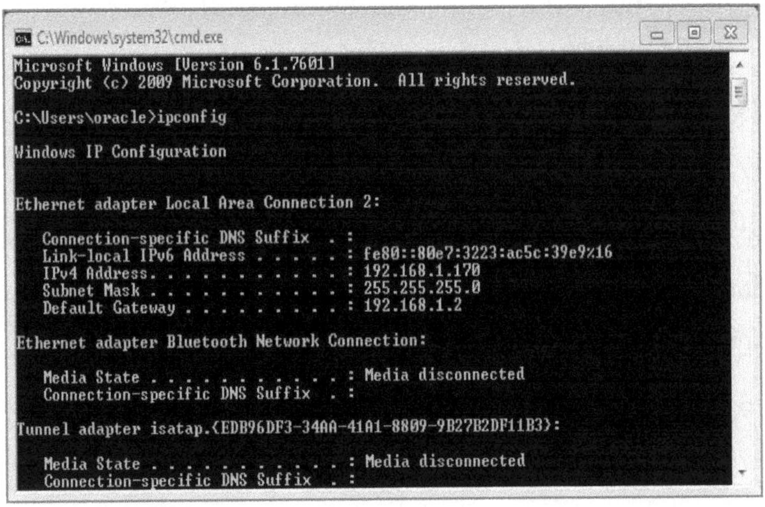

Figure 1.11

In figure 1.11, you can see the command line of Windows (**cmd**). Here's another example of an IP address:

10.0.0.1/24, where **/24** is the **network mask**

The **subnet mask** determines the **network size** (ex: how many devices can be connected to the same network, at the same time: for /28, there can be no more than 14 devices, in /25, there is a max of 126, for /24 a max of 254, etc.).

Below are the necessary **components** for an end device to **communicate** (connect) **successfully** on the Internet:

IP address = uniquely identifies a device connected to a network

Network Mask = determines the size of a network (ex: the number of available IP addresses)

Default Gateway = specifies the way out of the network (a Router connected to the Internet)

DNS Server = "transforms" a name (i.e. google.com) into an IP address (i.e. 173.23.85.91)

In the next chapter, we will talk about the OSI Model, a framework broken down into seven layers that explain precisely how the Internet (and communication) works.

Chapter 2

The OSI Model

The OSI model is a framework that defines the way devices communicate with the Internet (and in our LANs). This model is divided into **seven layers**, each independent of the other. Thus, changes may occur over time: new protocols and performance improvements at each layer without interfering with the functionality of the upper or the lower layer. The OSI model consists of 7 layers (you can also see the layers in Figure 2.1):

- **Physical**
- **Data Link**
- **Network**
- **Transport**
- **Session**
- **Presentation**
- **Application**

The OSI model helps us understand (in a more detailed way) how computer networks work and provides us with a better way of **troubleshooting** (solving problems that may occur in a network, regardless of its size) events.

Each layer defines how things should operate in the communication process of 2 or more devices. Each layer of the OSI model has its protocols that (all combined) define the behaviour of network devices.

For example, when we want to send traffic to a specific server, we need to know where to send that traffic (aka. the destination), so we're going to use the IP protocol (which works at Layer 3 - Network - we'll talk about it more in depth, later on). Another scenario could be a request to download a file or access a web page, in which case we're going to use protocols, such as FTP or HTTP.

And now maybe you're asking yourself: "hmm… protocol? what's a protocol ?" Well, it's simple:

A *protocol is a set of rules*. That's it! A set of rules for the way **devices behave** in a network.

As I said at the beginning of this chapter, most of the protocols are independent of each other. By designing things this way (thanks to the OSI model), no other protocols are affected in case of any changes. In Figure 2.1, below, you can see how the OSI model is structured:

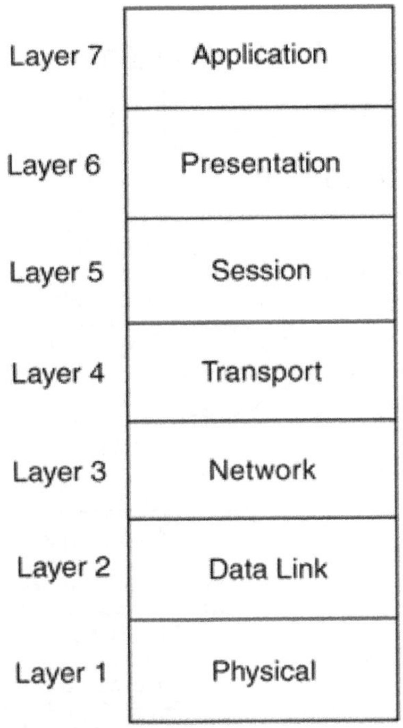

Layer 7	Application
Layer 6	Presentation
Layer 5	Session
Layer 4	Transport
Layer 3	Network
Layer 2	Data Link
Layer 1	Physical

Figure 2.1

As you can see in Figure 2.2, each layer is accompanied (on the left) by a component called **P**rotocol **D**ata **U**nit (**PDU**) or the data units that are being used by each layer:

- Layer 1 uses **Bits**
- Layer 2 uses **Frames**
- Layer 3 uses **Packets**
- Layer 4 uses **Segments** (or **Datagrams**)
- Layer 5 uses **Data**
- Layer 6 uses **Data**
- Layer 7 uses **Data**

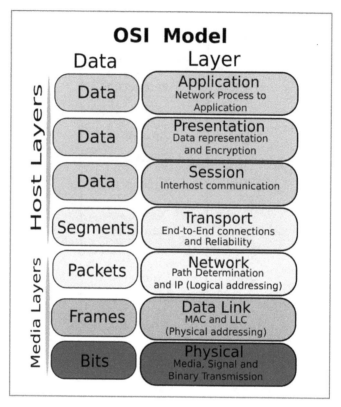

Figure 2.2

In the following chapters, we'll talk more about each layer of the OSI model, and you'll get a much clearer understanding of it. In figure 2.3, you can see a more in-depth example of the OSI model and (briefly) what each of its layers is all about:

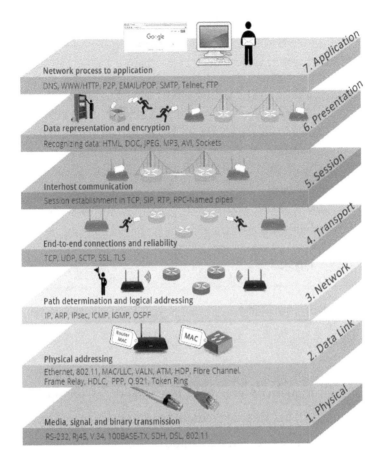

Figure 2.3

You have a concise breakdown of how things work for each layer. Don't worry. Starting with Chapter 3, we'll dive deep into each layer.

Now, I want to tell you that the OSI model is not alone. In "competition" with this model is the **TCP / IP model**, which was created and adopted faster (1974). Currently, this model is being used (Figure 2.4). The OSI model was first released in 1984, so there was a clear competitive advantage for the TCP/IP model.

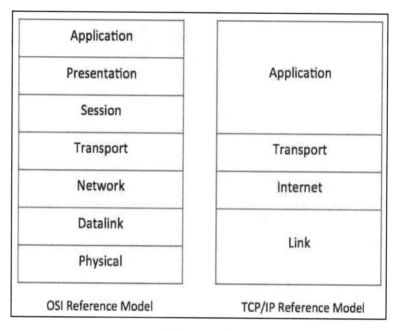

Figure 2.4

The TCP / IP model contains only **four layers** (as opposed to OSI's seven-layer model). Its first layer **includes** the two layers (Physical and Data Link) that are part of the OSI model. The last three layers (Application, Presentation and Session) are represented as a single layer in TCP / IP, namely Application. The purpose of these two models is to allow communication between 2 or more devices (on which different applications exist). When a PC wants to send a request for Google's homepage, it starts from the Application layer (the request being formatted in many streams of data) and moves down the OSI (or the TCP / IP) model till it reaches the Physical layer (and will be sent - in the format of the bits - as an electrical signal, light impulses or radio waves, down the cable). This process is known as **encapsulation.** The process in **reverse** is known as **decapsulation** (e.g., when the request reaches Google's web servers - (Physical Layer -> Application)

Chapter 3

Layer 1 – Physical

So, let's get into the OSI model and start with the 1ˢᵗ of its layers, the physical layer. When it comes to the **physical layer**, we will talk about the medium through which devices send information. The three main ways we can connect networks (and devices to networks) are:

- **Electrical** (UTP cable with eight small copper wires)
- **Light signal** (optical fiber)
- **Radio waves** (wireless)

The physical layer is the basis of computer networks because **it provides physical connectivity** between networks (or locations).

Each transmission medium has its advantages and disadvantages. For **example, wireless** over cable connection advantages are pretty straightforward: *mobility and flexibility*, while the disadvantages are *lower transfer speeds* and (lack of) *security*.

Instead, a **cable** connection (usually a UTP cable – we'll talk more in detail about it later) is much more *secure* and *reliable* than **wireless**. It can transport data at **much higher speed** rates (1/10/40 Gbps or more) and can be used over longer distances (up to 80 - 100 m on UTP).

The 2nd way we can transport data is by using light. Here come the **Optical Fiber** connections (which use light as a signaling method), which allow us to transport data over a longer distance (1 - 5 km or more) than the UTP cable (100 m) and at a much higher speed.

UTP Cable Types

Now, let's say that we (you and I) want to connect our laptops via a cable. Things mat very simply in this situation. You just take a cable and plug it into our laptops and everything will work just fine, isn't it? Well, it's not like this. A **UTP** (**U**nshielded **T**wisted **P**air) cable contains **eight small wires** (or pins), out of which four are being used to Send and 4 to Receive the traffic (as in figure 3.1):

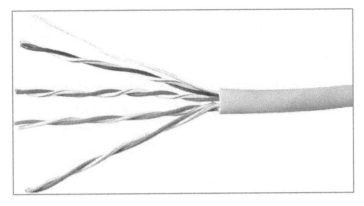

Figure 3.1

Also, there are many types of devices (PCs, Laptops, Routers, Switches, Access Points, Firewalls, etc.), and each of them requires a slightly different type of UTP cable.

The UTP cable has two ends that can be **plugged** in the following ways:

- **Straight** - the wires are the same at both ends
- **Crossover** - the wires are crossed at both ends
- **Rollover** - the wires are rolled over – (as in the console cable)

Each device stated above requires one type of UTP cable when connecting to another similar device. You will see what these cable types look like and what types to use for multiple devices on the next page.

Let's start with the **Straight** cable, which can be used to connect:

- Router to Switch
- Switch to PC
- Switch to Printer (or Server or any other end-device)

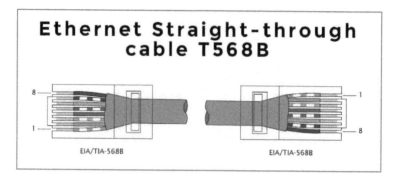

Figure 3.2

The following devices will use the **Crossover** cable to be connected:

- Switch to Switch
- Router to Router
- Router to PC
- PC to PC

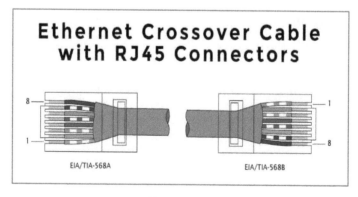

Figure 3.3

As you can see in the examples above (and as a general rule), we can say the **Straight** cable is used when **connecting different devices** (ex: Router

– Switch, Switch – PC, etc.), and the **Crossover** cable is used when **connecting similar devices** (ex: Router – Router, Switch – Switch, etc.). An exception to this rule has to do with the Router – PC (or Server) connection.

The Console Cable

Now let's move on and talk about the 3rd UTP cable type, which is the Rollover cable. When it comes to accessing (via the command line) a Router, we have two options:

- Connect directly to its **console port**
- **Remote access** via the network (by using **Telnet** or **SSH**)

If we want to connect to the equipment (Router, Switch, etc.) via the console, we need **physical access** to the device. In most cases, this is not possible. **At first**, when we set up from "zero," a brand new network device, we **must connect it to its console port.** This is because we don't have an IP address (on the equipment) to which we can connect remotely.

Also, we must use the console port when we lose access to the device (something happened with the network or with the equipment itself) because then we can investigate the incident (aka. troubleshoot).

We need a rollover cable to connect to any Cisco device through the console (see figure 3.4). This cable type will be inserted into a special port known as the **console port.**

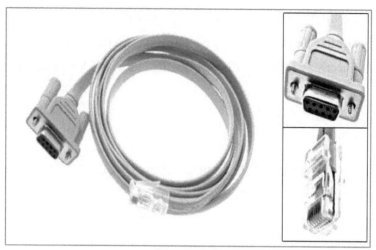

Figure 3.4

To **connect** to the Router (or Switch) **directly via console**, we also need a special program (such as **PuTTY** - in figure 3.5 below or TeraTerm, SecureCRT, etc.) that will give us access to the command line of the Router (or Switch) - as you can see in figure 3.6.

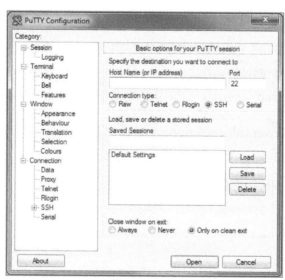

Figure 3.5

After completing this process, things will look similar to figure 3.6:

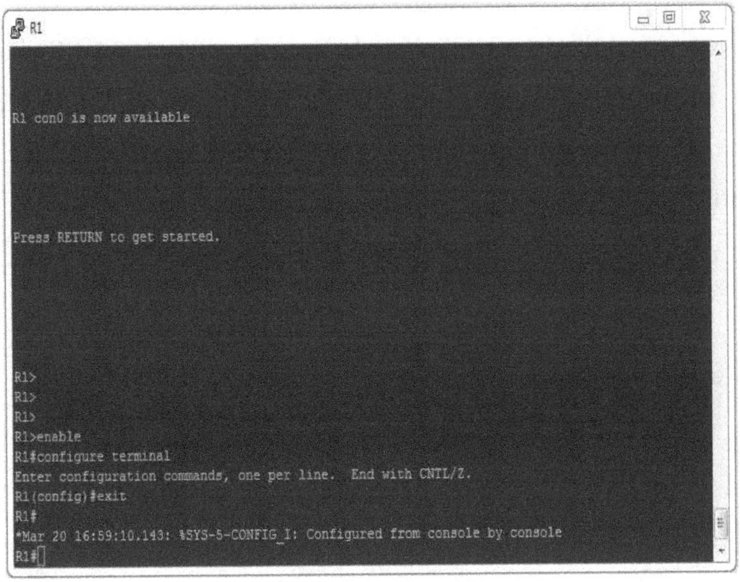

Figure 3.6

Ports, Interfaces and their speed

A port is a physical way to connect to the network (basically, it is the **physical part** and is "where the cable plugs in"). An interface is the **"logical" part** of the port (where we can **set an IP address**).

- In the port, we plug the (physical) cable
- On the interface, we set the IP address

For each port, the speed may differ. Depending on the model and the case, it can vary between 10 Mbps - and 100 Gbps (100,000 Mbps).

Mbps = Megabits per second

Gbps = Gigabits per second

The current standard in LANs (at the user level) is 1000 Mbps (or 1 Gbps). In Figure 3.7, you can see a Cisco Switch, which has 48 Gigabit Ethernet (1000 Mbps) ports and, on the right side, 4 x 10 Gigabit Ethernet ports.

Figure 3.7

It's normal for Switches to have a high port density (52 in this case, but other models have hundreds of ports) because **it is designed** to connect multiple devices in the same network (LAN).

Full-Duplex / Half-Duplex

Another important element of how a port works is how data is sent.

1. SW1 (and PC A) can send data by turn (the PC sends, the Switch just receives and vice versa: when the Switch sends, the PC receives - this process does **NOT happen simultaneously**) - this mode is known as **Half-Duplex**: Devices can **only** *send* **or** *receive*, but **NOT** at the same time (figure 3.8).

2. SW1 (and PC A) can send and receive data simultaneously - this mode is called **Full-Duplex** and is used in figure 3.9.

The benefit of using a **Full-Duplex** is straightforward: faster transfer speeds in the network.

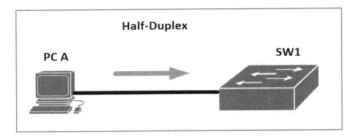

Figure 3.8

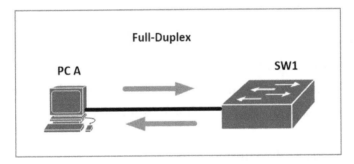

Figure 3.9

Collision domains and broadcast domains

A packet can reach different points in any network or conflict with other packets transmitted simultaneously: here, we'll be talking about the broadcast and collision domains.

1. Collision domains

A **collision** refers to the fact that two different devices simultaneously send a packet in the network. If the two packets are sent simultaneously, then a collision is formed. This is how network devices and PCs used to work at the beginning of the Internet (when technology was not as advanced as today).

In the early days of the Internet (the '80s - '90s), devices were operating in the half-duplex mode - a single device in the network was sending traffic at a given time, while the other devices connected to the same network had to wait for the first one to finish - to be able to send any traffic.

This was the way the networks operated in the 1990s and early 2000s. The collision-solving mechanism was CSMA / CD (Carrier Sense Multi Access with Collision Detection).

A collision can only occur on a **segment** (the connection between two devices: Switch - PC, PC - PC, Switch - Router, etc.) **half-duplex** from a network. Such collisions do not occur (or very rarely due to errors) because each device transmits the traffic in **full-duplex** mode.

2. Broadcast domains

A broadcast domain is a distance a packet (of a type of broadcast) can travel over the network. In other words, how far a broadcast packet can reach within a network will represent the broadcast domain.

In figure 3.11, you might wonder: *"Why is the connection between Routers a broadcast domain? Isn't that a collision domain ?"*

The answer is yes and yes. :) It's a broadcast domain because every **Router interface represents a new network** and a collision domain because it's a network segment. As we said earlier: a collision can occur on any network segment (usually half-duplex).

The images below (Figures 3.10 and 3.11) show the collision domains and the broadcast domains of network topology. As you can see in Figure 3.10, there are **four collision domains**:

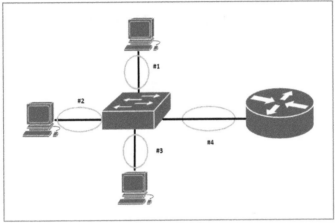

Figure 3.10

And in figure 3.10, there are **four broadcast domains**:

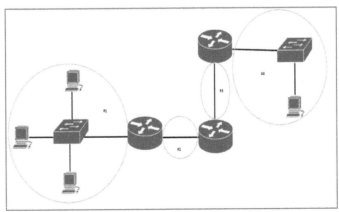

Figure 3.11

Chapter 4

Layer 2 - Data-Link

Basic Switching concepts

Moving forward to the 2nd layer of the OSI model, let's talk about Switches. So, what is a Switch? **A switch** is a network device running at **the 2nd layer of the OSI model**. Its **purpose** is to **interconnect** multiple devices (PCs, Laptops, Servers, Printers, etc.) into the **same** local area network (**LAN**). The Switch can do this because it contains multiple **ports** (**24** or **48** depending on the model) that allow other devices to connect to it via a UTP cable.

Figure 4.1

The vast majority of today's Switches use **Ethernet technology**. One of the reasons for Ethernet's widespread (and adoption) is its **superior data transfer speed/bandwidth** (1 Gbps / 10 Gbps / 40 Gbps or even 100 Gbps) as compared to other existing technologies (Token Ring, FDDI, etc.) that were available when Ethernet first came out.

Ethernet is extremely useful because it lets the Switch know where to send data from one device to another (**based on the MAC addresses** - source and destination). A **MAC address** is a **unique identifier** for each device connected to a network. This address is **written on the NIC** (Network Interface Card) of every single device by the vendor that manufactures it (ex: Intel, Broadcom, TP-Link, etc.).

In figure 4.2, you will be able to see a representation of the MAC address from the command line of Windows. You can find your MAC address by clicking "**Start**" -> (type) **cmd** -> (then type the command) "**ipconfig /all**"

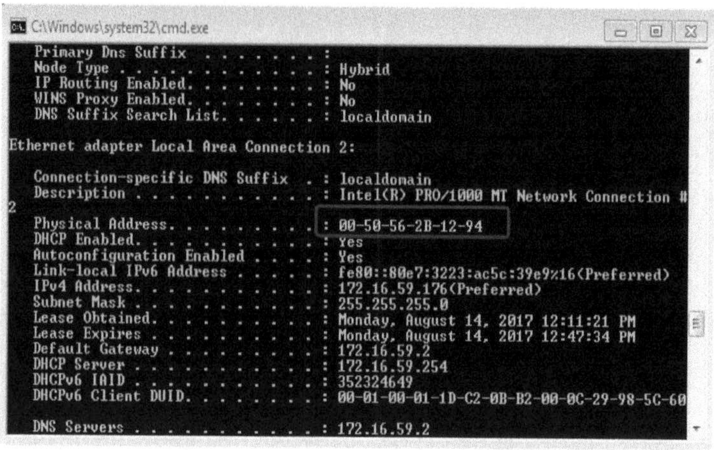

Figure 4.2

The MAC address from figure 4.2 is 00-50-56-2B-12-94 and is represented in hexadecimal format, **48 bits** (12 characters, 4 bits per character). The **first 24 bits** (00-50-56) represent the "**vendor** ID" (ex. Cisco, Apple, Intel, etc.), and the next 24 bits (2B-12-94) represent the **device-specific part** that uniquely identifies a device in a network.

What is Ethernet?

I'm pretty sure that you've heard about Ethernet before. Why? Because:

1. I've mentioned it earlier
2. And because your home Router uses this technology (just like your PC or Laptop) – just take a look at the NIC - network interface

Today, **Ethernet** is the most widespread network technology, mainly due to the following characteristics:

- **Higher transfer speeds** (10/40/100 Gigabit per second)
- **The Way of identifying** (addressing) **devices** (**MAC** addresses) in a network

Today's Routers and Switches all use the Ethernet standard (on their ports). These ports can be **labeled** by using one of the following speed rates:

- **Fast Ethernet** - 100Mbps (aka. Fa0/1 ... Fa0/24)
- **Gigabit Ethernet** - 1000Mbps (aka. Gi0/1 ... Gi0/24)
- **Ten Gigabit Ethernet** - 10000Mbps (aka. TenGi0/1 ... TenGi0/24)

Thus, as the devices send traffic to the network, **the Switch will learn their source (MAC)** address and **associate** them with the **ports** they come from (the port on which the device is connected - ex: Fa0/1, Fa0/10, or Gi0/4, etc.)

In figure 4.3, you can see what the **Ethernet header** looks like:

8 bytes	6 bytes	6 bytes	2 bytes	46-1500 bytes	4 bytes
Preamble	Destination Address	Source Address	Type Field	Data	Frame Check Sequence (FCS)

Figure 4.3

Let's talk a little bit more in detail about each component of the Ethernet header:

1. **Preamble** - a string of bits that indicates the beginning of a frame
2. **Destination Address** - the destination MAC address
3. **Source Address** - the source MAC address
4. **Type Field** - Indicates the Ethernet version being used and the length of the frame
5. **Data** - represents the actual transmitted data (together with the upper layer headers)
6. **FCS** - way of checking the integrity of the frame (frame sent = frame received)
7. **EOF** (End of Frame bits) - series of special bits indicating the frame termination (not in the figure)

Now, let's see how the Ethernet header looks in a Wireshark packet capture (figure 4.4):

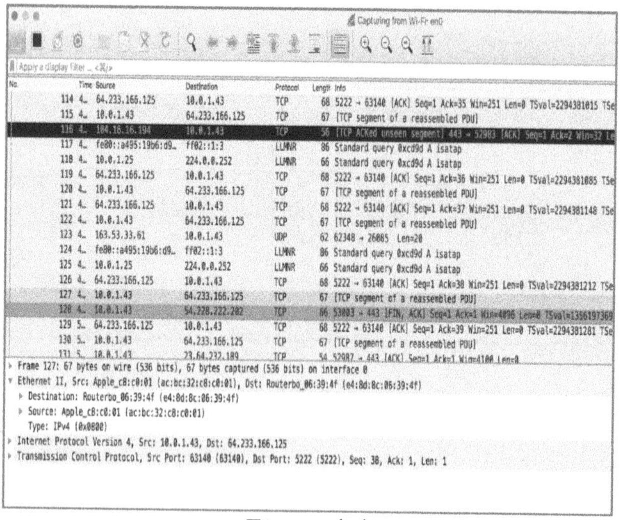

Figure 4.4

Wireshark is a cool tool. It's a program that lets us see the network traffic being generated by our machine (laptop, PC, server, etc.). In Figure 4.4, you can see how the communication between our device and other devices from the Internet (or LAN) works. Although it can be overwhelming at first, bear with me, as we will focus only on one packet (or data stream).

As you can see, I've selected (grey line) a random data stream that allows us to see even deeper into the packet. Here's what we can identify from the lower part of the image:

- TCP data stream between 2 devices (more about it in chapter 6)
- IP addresses (more about it in chapter 5)
- **Ethernet II**, where you can easily identify the **2 MAC addresses** (destination and source).

Now that we've talked about Ethernet let's move on and talk about how Switches and the switching process work.

How do Switches learn and use MAC addresses?

The **purpose** of a **Switch is to interconnect multiple devices** in the same network (LAN). It does this by using **MAC addresses** (source and destination).

The **destination MAC** address is used to identify and send traffic to a device from the network (aka. the destination), while the **source MAC** address stores **the port** on which a device is located.

So practically, the Switch **learns** about each device in the network based on its **source MAC address** and decides where to send the information based on the *destination MAC address.*

The **Switch keeps** all of the information in a special memory known as the **CAM** (**C**ontent-**A**ddressable **M**emory) table. This **CAM table** describes the MAC address (source) on a port (in other words, it makes a port mapping/association MAC address - example: The MAC address X is on the Fa0 / 5 port, MAC address G is on port Fa0 / 9).

Let's take the topology network of Figure 4.5 in which 3 PCs are linked to a Switch:

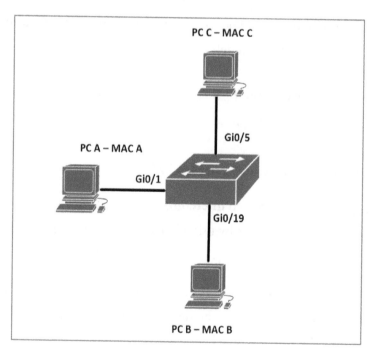

Figure 4.5

The CAM table of the Switch from Figure 4.5 will look (in the beginning) like this:

ID	MAC Addresses	Port
1		Gi0/1
2		Gi0/19
3		Gi0/5

Table 4.1

As you can see in table 4.1, the CAM table is empty in the beginning (immediately after boot). In other words, **the Switch doesn't know the MAC addresses** of the connected devices.

Imagine that the 3 PCs from figure 4.5 are starting to communicate over the network. How are they going to do it? What's going to happen with the Switch? What is it going to do?

In the following steps (1 - 5) and tables, you'll be able to see how the Switching process works. So let's see:

1) PC A sends the message to PC B

The **Switch** will **learn PC A's MAC** address on port Gi0/1.

ID	MAC Addresses	Port
1	A	Gi0/1
2		Gi0/19
3		Gi0/5

The Switch **sends the message** as a **broadcast** because it doesn't know which port PC B is connected to.

2) PC B receives the message

ID	MAC Addresses	Port
1	A	Gi0/1
2		Gi0/19
3		Gi0/5

3) PC B replies to PC A

The Switch learns the MAC address of PC B and sends the message (based on his CAM table) to PC A on port Gi0/1.

ID	MAC Addresses	Port
1	A	Gi0/1
2	B	Gi0/19
3		Gi0/5

4) PC B sends a message to PC C

The Switch **sends the message** as a **broadcast** because it doesn't know which port PC C (MAC address) is.

ID	MAC Addresses	Port
1	A	GiO/1
2	B	GiO/19
3		GiO/5

5) PC C replies to PC B

The Switch learns the MAC address of PC C and sends the message (based on its CAM table) to PC B.

ID	MAC Addresses	Port
1	A	GiO/1
2	B	GiO/19
3	C	GiO/5

Now, in this stage, the Switch knows every MAC address from the network. If any other devices joined the network, the **process** would **repeat** for any **unknown** (by the Switch) MAC address. If any devices stopped sending traffic for more than 300 seconds (**5 minutes**), the Switch would **flush** its **MAC** address from the CAM table.

Besides the Ethernet standard, other standards/protocols work on **the 2nd layer of the OSI model** (I'm just going to mention them):

- **PPP** (Point-to-Point Protocol)
- **PPPoE** (Point-to-Point Protocol over Ethernet) - used by ISPs for its authentication feature
- **MPLS** - the current protocol/standard for organizations to connect their sites via the ISP (Internet Service Provider

Chapter 5

Layer 3 – Network

Basic Routing concepts

As you can see, the **MAC** address is **only used** for communication within the local network. For example, it is used when 2 PCs send traffic between each other on the LAN. If they would try to communicate on the Internet, then an **IP address** (and a Router) would be required.

The purpose of a **Router** (figure 5.1 - Cisco 2811 model) is to **connect multiple networks** (e.g., LAN) into a larger network (often called a WAN - Wide Area Network). Thus, the Router's main purpose is to make a simple decision for every single packet that comes in:

"On what interface should I send this packet? And if I don't know where to send it, I'll drop it. "

Figure 5.1

By knowing multiple network locations, a Router can send the traffic from one network to the other. Moving the traffic forward towards its destinations is known as **routing**.

ATTENTION! By default, a **Router** only **knows its Directly Connected** networks. It does not know how to send packets further. This is where we, the administrators, come in. We'll have to tell the Router which way to reach the destination.

When Routers boot up, they **first learn** about their **directly connected networks** (those starting with C in Figure 5.2). In figure 5.2, you can see the routing table of a Cisco Router, which contains the directly connected networks (C) and the IP address of R1 on those interfaces (L).

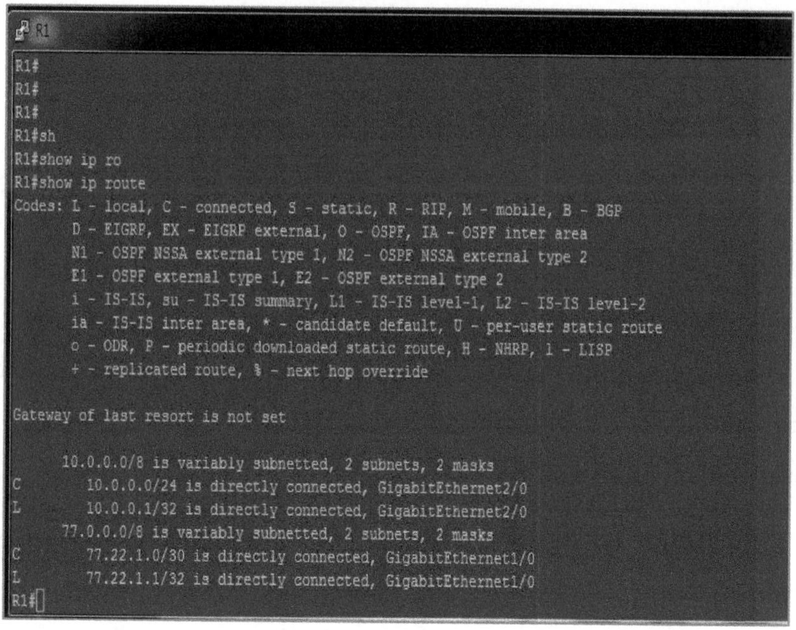

Figure 5.2

Making the routing process possible, the Router uses the **destination IP address** as a reference point (*"to whom should the traffic be sent?"* - the **destination**) and the source IP address as the **source** (*"from where did the traffic come from?"*).

To send the traffic (packets) to its destination, the Router needs to know, first of all, the destination. This can be done if the **Router learns** how to reach that destination, a process that can be achieved in one of 2 ways:

- **Manual** - via Static Routes
- **Dynamic** - via Routing Protocols (RIP, OSPF, EIGRP)

We will start talking about the **IPv4** and **IPv6** protocols (and addresses) in the following sections. In Chapter 8, we'll move on to the practical side and configure a Cisco Router in the network simulator Cisco Packet Tracer.

What is IPv4?

The **IPv4 protocol** was developed in the 1980s and it was designed to use **32 bits** of data to define an IP address (ex: **192.168.1.1**). As you can see in the example 192.168.1.1, there are four fields separated by dots and each field of these four can be allocated 8 bits of data:

8 bits * **4** fields = **32** bits.

Now, let's think about this number of bits, 32. It can tell us something about the maximum number of IP addresses that can be generated: 2 ^ 32 ~= **4.3 Billion**!

Yeah, you read it well, 4.3 billion IPv4 addresses.

TIP: why 2 ^ 32? Because each bit can be 0 or 1, if we have 32 bits, we can generate about 4.3 billion unique numbers/addresses.

In 2011, in the summer of that year, **IANA** (Internet **A**ssigned **N**umbers **A**uthority) allocated the last IPv4 address space. Does that mean we can't connect other devices to the Internet anymore? Not at all. Since then, the Internet has grown a lot. Here's a graph (figure 5.3) that predicts the growth of the Internet in terms of the connected devices:

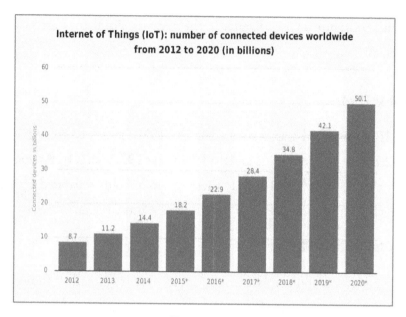

Figure 5.3

NOTE: Please note that there is a difference between **allocated and used**. IANA has provided all of its available IP addresses to the Service Providers (ISP) worldwide. Still, these addresses are far from being USED by the ISP (or, more exactly, used by us, the consumers).

As I said earlier, the maximum number of IPv4 addresses is **~4.3 Billion**.

In 2016, it was estimated that the **total number** of **devices connected** to the **Internet** would be around **~20 billion**, exceeding the IPv4 address number.

Due to this problem, measures have been taken to **slow IPv4 address** allocation by using techniques such as NAT and introducing the concept of *Public and Private IP*. To another extent, far better than NAT is the introduction of the **IPv6 protocol**, which we will discuss a little bit later.

The Structure of an IPv4 Packet

In figure 5.4, you can see the structure (header) of an IPv4 packet

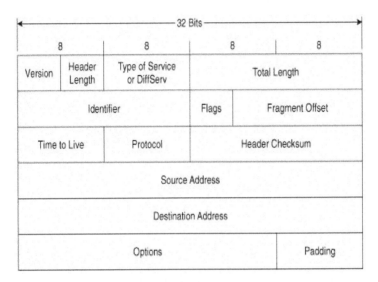

Figure 5.4

Here, we can identify some important components that we'll interact within many situations throughout our IT studies/career:

- **IP Source Address**
- **IP Destination Address**
- **TTL** (Time to Live)
- **ToS (T**ype of Service)
- **Header Checksum**

Now, let's talk about each of these in more detail, and let's start with the IP addresses. I assume that it's clear that in any communication between 2 devices, we need a *source address* and a *destination address*.

The two fields (Source & Destination Address) are reserved for the **source and destination IP addresses**.

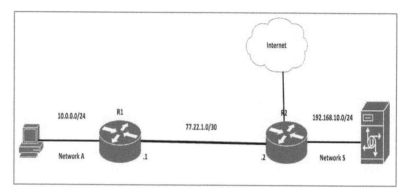

Figure 5.5

For example, in Figure 5.5, you can see the two networks: A and S. If the PC from Network A (with the IP 10.0.0.5) wants to communicate with the server (with the IP 192.168.10.8) from network S, then the source address of each packet will be **10.0.0.5** (PC's IP), and the destination address will be **192.168.10.8** (Server's IP).

IPv4 Classes

As I said at the beginning of this chapter, each field (4 in total) of an IP address can have any value between **0 - 255** (8 bits/field, so 256 values, $2 \wedge 8 = 256$). Thus, IP addresses are divided into several classes:

IP Class	Start IP	End IP	Network Prefix
A	1.0.0.0	127.255.255.255	1 - 127
B	128.0.0.0	191.255.255.255	128 - 191
C	192.0.0.0	223.255.255.255	192 - 223
D	224.0.0.0	239.255.255.255	224 - 239
E	240.0.0.0	255.255.255.255	240 - 255

Classes A, B and C are **used on the Internet**, Class D is reserved for multicast addresses, and Class E is an experimental class that is not being used.

Public IP vs. Private IP

Public IP addresses, as their name says, are being used to communicate (transit) over the (Public) Internet, and the **Private IP** addresses are used in Local Area Networks (**LANs**) such as our home network or our school's network.

Thus, **Private IP addresses will never reach the Internet**. For us to be able to communicate over the Internet, a protocol such as **NAT** (Network Address Translation) will be created to transform *Private IPs into Public IPs*.

Private IP Addresses

In the table below are the ranges of the Private IP addresses out there:

IP Class	Start IP	IP End	Network Prefix
A	10.0.0.1	10.255.255.255	10.0.0.0/8
B	172.16.0.1	172.31.255.255	172.16.0.0/12
C	192.168.0.1	192.168.255.255	192.168.0.0/16

NOTE: The rest of the IP addresses not mentioned in this table are PUBLIC!

Thus, we can have a scenario similar to figure 5.6 below (multiple LANs - Network A and S - which contain private IP addresses and public IP addresses for the rest of the networks).

Also, these Private IP addresses (with the help of NAT) improve our **network's security**, making it harder for potential attackers to enter it.

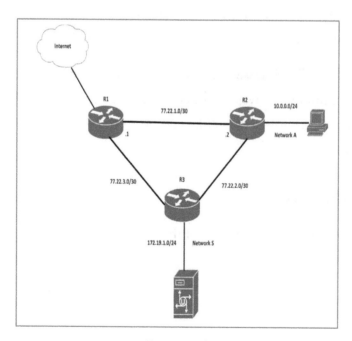

Figure 5.6

Three ways of sending Packets in the Network

Have you ever thought of how end devices or network devices send the packets in the network? Well, here are the three options available out there:

Unicast

Multicast

Broadcast

In the **Unicast mode**, communication between 2 devices is **1 to 1**. This means there is a single source and a single destination. Think of unicast as talking to a friend (you're addressing yourself to only one person).

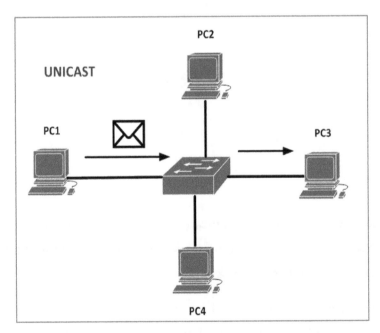

Figure 5.7

In **Multicast mode**, the communication between devices is **1 to many** (a specific group of devices). Imagine that you are in a room with 100 people, and you only have a conversation with a group of 10 people/colleagues (aka specific group). This is multicast.

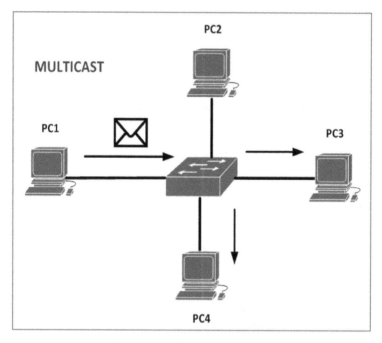

Figure 5.8

In **Broadcast mode**, the communication between devices is *1 to N* (where *N* represents all devices in the network). **Broadcast traffic is intended for every device in the network.**

Once again, imagine you are in the same room with 100 people; you are on a stage and talking to everyone. This is the equivalent of the broadcast.

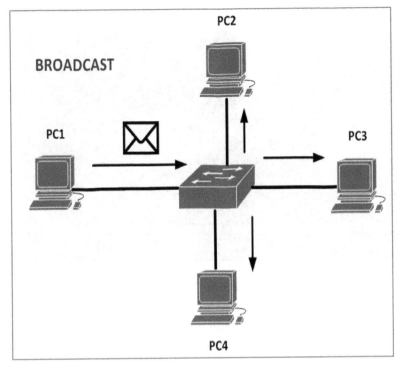

Figure 5.9

Configuring an IP address on Windows 7/8/10

On Windows, when it comes to setting up an IP address, we have two options: from the command line or the GUI. First, we'll start by checking our IP address from the command line:

```
C:\Windows\system32\cmd.exe

Microsoft Windows [Version 6.1.7601]
Copyright (c) 2009 Microsoft Corporation.  All rights reserved.

C:\Users\oracle>ipconfig

Windows IP Configuration

Ethernet adapter Local Area Connection 2:

   Connection-specific DNS Suffix  . :
   Link-local IPv6 Address . . . . . : fe80::80e7:3223:ac5c:39e9%16
   IPv4 Address. . . . . . . . . . . : 192.168.1.170
   Subnet Mask . . . . . . . . . . . : 255.255.255.0
   Default Gateway . . . . . . . . . : 192.168.1.2

Ethernet adapter Bluetooth Network Connection:

   Media State . . . . . . . . . . . : Media disconnected
   Connection-specific DNS Suffix  . :

Tunnel adapter isatap.{EDB96DF3-34AA-41A1-8809-9B27B2DF11B3}:

   Media State . . . . . . . . . . . : Media disconnected
   Connection-specific DNS Suffix  . :
```

Figure 5.10

The command used in figure 5.10 is **>ipconfig** and as you can see, it shows us more information about the Ethernet (LAN), Wi-Fi, and Bluetooth adapters. The most important elements shown by the command's output are:

- *IPv4 Address*
- *Network Mask*
- *Default gateway*
- *IPv6 Address*

All of these elements can be configured in one of two ways:

- **Statically** - we'll assign all of the info manually
- **Dynamically** - a protocol (such as DHCP) was configured on a server and assigned dynamic IP addresses with no human interaction at all.

Okay, now let's see how we can configure all of the above elements on Windows 7 (8.1 or 10). In figures 5.11 and 5.12, you'll be able to see how we can do this:

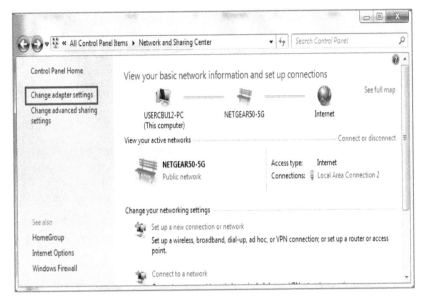

Figure 5.11

A very simple way to configure a **static IP address** is to go to the "**Control Panel -> Network and Sharing Center**" first, followed by "**Change adapter settings**" (or **Network and Internet -> Network Connections**). Now you'll reach a window similar to the one shown in the figure 5.12:

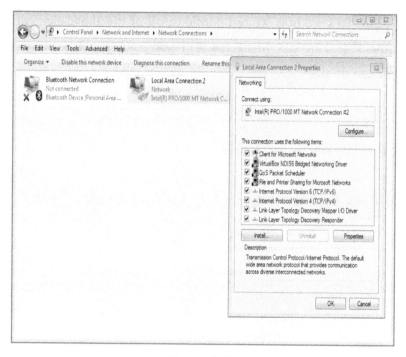

Figure 5.12

Here, we are looking for the "**Local Area Connection 2**" (in your case might be a similar name), and **right-click** on it, followed by **"Properties"**. A new window will open, from which we'll **select IPv4** and then **click on Properties**.

At this point, we have reached a similar window to the one in figure 5.13. Here, we can (finally) set *the IP address, the Subnet Mask, Default Gateway and the DNS Server.*

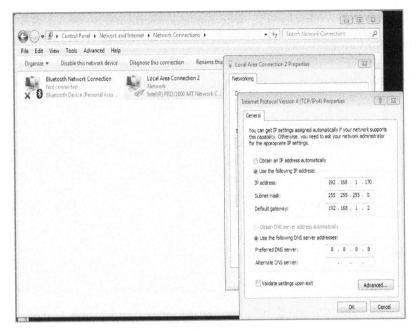

Figure 5.13

For this example, let's choose a network from which we'll select the other elements required to access the Internet. The network's IP address will be 192.168.1.0/24, out of which **192.168.1.170** will be assigned to the PC (Windows 7). The **/24** in decimal mask looks 255.255.255.0 and the **default gateway** (the Internet-connected Router) will have the IP address of 192.168.1.2.

We also need to set the **DNS** server (the one that helps us with the name resolution: from a domain (ex: google.com) will provide us with its IP address (ex: 216.58.214.227)) of **8.8.8.8**

Now that we're done with all of these settings, we can check our configuration (from CMD) using the following commands:

>**ping 8.8.8.8**   //checks the Internet connection(actually to 8.8.8.8, which is a Google's server)

>**ping google.com**   //checks the DNS service **and** the Internet connection

>**nslookup google.com** //checks the DNS service

In the next section, we'll start talking about the successor of IPv4, the "new" **IPv6** protocol.

What is IPv6?

Today, there are more than 20 billion devices connected to the Internet worldwide, and the number keeps getting bigger and bigger as days pass by. This is a major problem, especially for ISPs (Internet Service Providers), because it exceeds the 4.3 Billion that IPv4 was providing.

So here comes the need for a better, much larger protocol, known as IPv6. IPv6 is a new addressing (identification) protocol that introduces a new address format (in hexadecimal) and a much, much larger addressing space.

IPv6 is 128 bits long (that means we have 2two^ 128 addresses available), which is an infinitely large space compared to IPv4whichat is only 32 bits long). Besides these features, IPv6 will streamline the communication process of devices on the Internet, making everything faster and more secure. According to <u>Wikipedia</u>, this number looks like this:

"340,282,366,920,938,463,463,374,607,431,768,211,456 or 3.4×10^{38} (340 <u>trillions</u> of trillions of trillions)"

Figure 5.14

Here are a few examples of IPv6 addresses:

- **2001:DB8:85A3:8D45:119:8C2A:370:734B /64**
- **FE80::C001:37FF:FE6C:0/64**
- **2001::1/128**

As you can see, IPv6 addresses are represented in the **hexadecimal format** (it includes the **digits 0-9** and **letters A-F**). An IPv6 address is comprised of up to **8 fields** and a network mask (indicating how large the network is - the number of addresses).

Notes: Each IPv6 address field is separated by "**:**", but there can be a few exceptions:

2002:ABCD:1234:BBBA:0000:0000:0000:0001/64 can also be written in the following ways:

    a.   2002:ABCD:1234:BBBA**:0:0:0:**1/64

    b.   2002:ABCD:1234:BBBA::1/64

If we want to **reduce** a whole **integer of 0s**, we will simplify it by "**::**". **ATTENTION!** "::" can be **used** only **once**.

In Figure 5.15 below, you can see an IPv6 address (command **>ipconfig**) from CMD that begins with the notation of **FE80:**...

This **IPv6 address** is **special** because it can only be used in the local area network (**LAN**) to communicate with other devices.

This type of address is a **Local Link** generated automatically (another important feature of IPv6 - address auto-configuration).

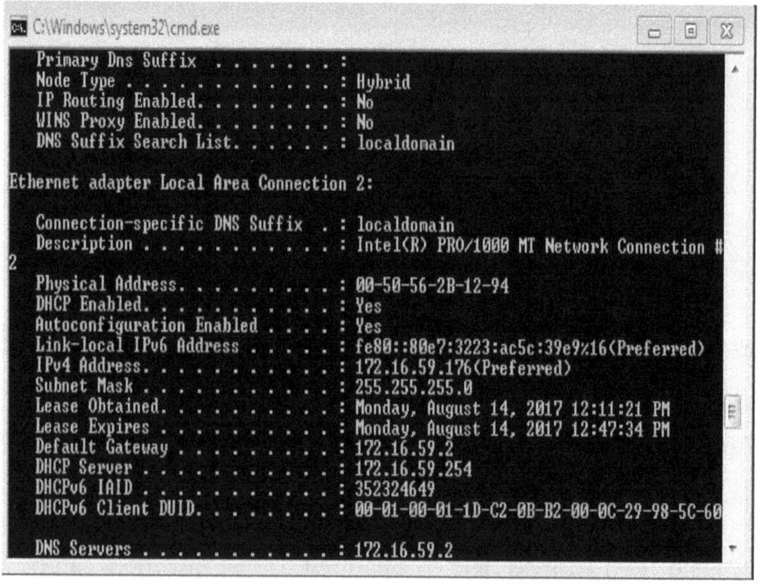

Figure 5.15

Chapter 6

Layer 4 – Transport

1) TCP

TCP comes from **T**ransmission **C**ontrol **P**rotocol, and it does what it says: ensures the transmission control of every single path in a communication channel.

It can be found (together with UDP) on the 4th layer of the OSI model, which is the Transport layer. As a PDU (Protocol Data Unit), **TCP uses segments** (it breaks the data into smaller pieces known as segments).

TCP is a protocol that's being used (by you, me and everyone else on the Internet) all the time (without us even being aware of it). That's because it does a great job of keeping this seamless.

For example, when we download a file from the Internet, access a web page, or **connect to a network device**, we use the TCP protocol.

Now comes the question: **Why? Why do we need it?** Because TCP allows us to communicate by sharing the exact data (ex: web page) that the server or the client has. So when we download a file (through FTP), the TCP will ensure that **each segment** composing the file (located on the server) will be received. In case of missing segments, everything will be retransmitted.

So here are some of the features and benefits of the TCP protocol:

- **Retransmission** of data (in case it's being "lost on the road")
- **Packet reordering**
- **Establishes a connection** between the client and the server (3-way handshake)

TCP achieves the elements mentioned above by using the following message types:

- **SYN, ACK, FIN**
- **PSH, RST, URG**

We'll talk more about them in the following sections. Now let's see how TCP works. In figure 6.1, you can see the **TCP header structure:**

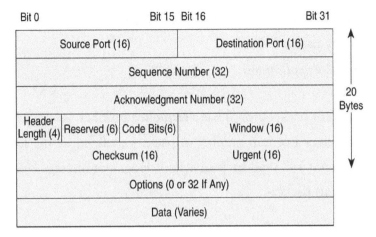

Figure 6.1

And in figure 6.2, you can see it in a **Wireshark capture:**

```
> Ethernet II, Src: IntelCor_22:69:1f (e4:a7:a0:22:69:1f), Dst: All-HSRP-routers_50 (00:00:0c:07:ac:50)
> Internet Protocol Version 4, Src: 10.84.166.102, Dst: 10.92.32.10
⊿ Transmission Control Protocol, Src Port: 64806 (64806), Dst Port: 80 (80), Seq: 0, Len: 0
    Source Port: 64806
    Destination Port: 80
    [Stream index: 109]
    [TCP Segment Len: 0]
    Sequence number: 0    (relative sequence number)
    Acknowledgment number: 0
    Header Length: 32 bytes
  ⊳ Flags: 0x002 (SYN)
    Window size value: 8192
    [Calculated window size: 8192]
  ⊳ Checksum: 0x2213 [validation disabled]
    Urgent pointer: 0
  ⊳ Options: (12 bytes) Maximum segment size, No-Operation (NOP), Window scale, No-Operation (NOP), No-Operation (NOP), SACK permitted
```

Figure 6.2

Having all of these fields in the protocol header, TCP can provide us with:

- *Data reordering*

- *Data retransmission* is done by using **sequence numbers** (in case of any packet being lost)
- *Reliable applications*

Each packet (or packet group) has a **sequence number** associated. If the recipient receives a certain number of packets (defined by the sequence number), then it will send back an acknowledgment message (ACK) for those (received) packets:

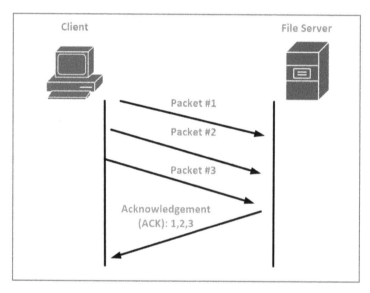

Figure 6.3

Thus, it's easy for the recipient to figure out what packets have reached and what packets need to be retransmitted. If the source (client) does not receive an ACK for any packets, it will retransmit those packets.

At first, when two devices want to communicate via a client-server connection, a **3-Way Handshake** session must be established.

How does a Client establish a connection to a Server?

As I said earlier, when a server has to communicate with a client, the two will form a connection between them. This connection is known as the **3-Way Handshake**. Now, let's take a look at how this handshake takes place:

At first, the client (the one who starts the connection) will send to the server:

1. a synchronization message (**SYN**) - marking the beginning of a session
2. The server will respond with an acknowledgment (**SYN-ACK**)
3. The client will also respond to the server with an acknowledgment (**ACK**)

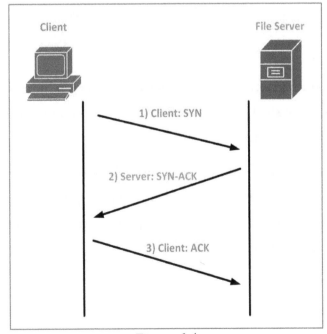

Figure 6.4

Here's a Wireshark capture with the three packets shown above:

No.	Time	Source	Destination	Protocol	Length	Info
824	13.447890	172.217.22.35	172.20.10.2	TCP	54	443 → 60072 [ACK] Seq=327296 Ack=4913 Win=68224 Len=0
825	13.448051	172.217.22.35	172.20.10.2	TCP	54	443 → 60072 [ACK] Seq=327296 Ack=4955 Win=68224 Len=0
826	13.448118	172.217.22.35	172.20.10.2	TCP	54	443 → 60072 [ACK] Seq=327296 Ack=5336 Win=69888 Len=0
827	13.463972	172.217.22.35	172.20.10.2	TLSv1.2	124	Application Data
828	13.464270	172.217.22.35	172.20.10.2	TLSv1.2	100	Application Data
829	13.464450	172.20.10.2	172.217.22.35	TCP	54	60072 → 443 [ACK] Seq=5336 Ack=327412 Win=301312 Len=0
830	13.468114	172.217.22.35	172.217.22.35	TLSv1.2	100	Application Data
831	13.471701	172.217.22.35	172.20.10.2	TLSv1.2	130	Application Data
832	13.472108	172.217.22.35	172.20.10.2	TLSv1.2	375	Application Data
833	13.472321	172.20.10.2	172.217.22.35	TCP	54	60072 → 443 [ACK] Seq=5382 Ack=327809 Win=301056 Len=0
834	13.472600	172.217.22.35	172.20.10.2	TLSv1.2	250	Application Data
835	13.563104	172.217.22.35	172.20.10.2	TCP	54	443 → 60072 [ACK] Seq=328005 Ack=5382 Win=69888 Len=0
836	13.626283	172.20.10.1	172.20.10.2	DNS	178	Standard query response 0x34c6 A www.theuselessweb.com
837	13.628302	172.20.10.2	52.216.17.122	TCP	66	60082 → 80 [SYN] Seq=0 Win=8192 Len=0 MSS=1260 WS=256 S
838	13.634831	172.20.10.2	52.216.17.122	TCP	66	60083 → 80 [SYN] Seq=0 Win=8192 Len=0 MSS=1260 WS=256 S
839	13.655255	52.216.17.122	172.20.10.2	TCP	66	80 → 60082 [SYN, ACK] Seq=0 Ack=1 Win=14600 Len=0 MSS=1
840	13.655423	172.20.10.2	52.216.17.122	TCP	54	60082 → 80 [ACK] Seq=1 Ack=1 Win=66560 Len=0
841	13.656092	172.20.10.2	52.216.17.122	HTTP	505	GET / HTTP/1.1
842	13.659177	52.216.17.122	172.20.10.2	TCP	66	80 → 60083 [SYN, ACK] Seq=0 Ack=1 Win=14600 Len=0 MSS=1
843	13.659330	172.20.10.2	52.216.17.122	TCP	54	60083 → 80 [ACK] Seq=1 Ack=1 Win=66560 Len=0
844	13.665985	172.20.10.2	172.217.22.35	TCP	54	60072 → 443 [ACK] Seq=5382 Ack=328005 Win=300800 Len=0
845	13.699258	52.216.17.122	172.20.10.2	TCP	54	80 → 60082 [ACK] Seq=1 Ack=452 Win=15872 Len=0
846	14.074045	172.20.10.2	239.255.255.250	SSDP	216	M-SEARCH * HTTP/1.1

> Frame 838: 66 bytes on wire (528 bits), 66 bytes captured (528 bits) on interface 0
> Ethernet II, Src: IntelCor_22:69:1f (e4:a7:a0:22:69:1f), Dst: 3a:65:90:d5:71:64 (3a:65:90:d5:71:64)
> Internet Protocol Version 4, Src: 172.20.10.2, Dst: 52.216.17.122
> Transmission Control Protocol, Src Port: 60083 (60083), Dst Port: 80 (80), Seq: 0, Len: 0

Figure 6.5

The **TCP connection** (via **3-way handshake**) between the client and the server was **established**. Now the two devices can communicate (send web traffic, transfer files, etc.).

This mechanism of the 3-way handshake helps ensure the client and the server that all packets are being counted (sequenced), ordered and verified at their destination. In case some of the packets are missing, they will be resent (by the sender).

How does TCP terminate a connection?

After all, packets have been transmitted, and the connection must end. This is similar to a 3-way handshake, but this time four packets are being sent:

1. **the client** sends a **FIN** packet
2. **the server** responds with an acknowledgment (**FIN-ACK**)
3. **the server** also sends a **FIN** message
4. **the client** replies with an acknowledgment, **FIN-ACK**

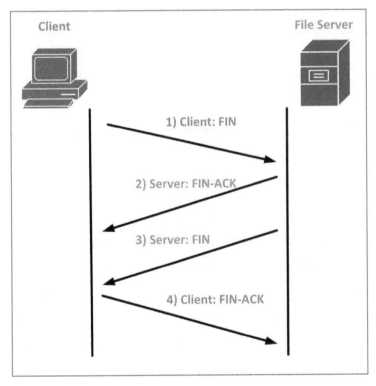

Figure 6.6

Here's the Wireshark capture with the concepts discussed above:

No.	Time	Source	Destination	Protocol	Length	Info
3486	-165.344927	10.92.32.10	10.84.166.102	TCP	1314	[TCP segment of a reassembled PDU]
3487	-165.344829	10.92.32.10	10.84.166.102	TCP	1314	[TCP segment of a reassembled PDU]
3488	-165.344813	10.84.166.102	10.92.32.10	TCP	54	64806 → 80 [ACK] Seq=240 Ack=41154 Win=66560 Len=0
3489	-165.344151	10.92.32.10	10.84.166.102	TCP	1314	[TCP segment of a reassembled PDU]
3490	-165.344117	10.92.32.10	10.84.166.102	TCP	1314	[TCP segment of a reassembled PDU]
3491	-165.343983	10.84.166.102	10.92.32.10	TCP	54	64806 → 80 [ACK] Seq=240 Ack=43674 Win=66560 Len=0
3492	-165.343918	10.92.32.10	10.84.166.102	TCP	1314	[TCP segment of a reassembled PDU]
3493	-165.343905	10.92.32.10	10.84.166.102	TCP	1314	[TCP segment of a reassembled PDU]
3494	-165.343896	10.84.166.102	10.92.32.10	TCP	54	64806 → 80 [ACK] Seq=240 Ack=46194 Win=66560 Len=0
3495	-165.343861	10.92.32.10	10.84.166.102	TCP	1314	[TCP segment of a reassembled PDU]
3496	-165.343780	10.92.32.10	10.84.166.102	TCP	1314	[TCP segment of a reassembled PDU]
3497	-165.343771	10.84.166.102	10.92.32.10	TCP	54	64806 → 80 [ACK] Seq=240 Ack=48714 Win=66560 Len=0
3498	-165.343721	10.92.32.10	10.84.166.102	TCP	1314	[TCP segment of a reassembled PDU]
3499	-165.343708	10.92.32.10	10.84.166.102	TCP	1314	[TCP segment of a reassembled PDU]
3500	-165.343641	10.84.166.102	10.92.32.10	TCP	54	64806 → 80 [ACK] Seq=240 Ack=51234 Win=66560 Len=0
3501	-165.343605	10.92.32.10	10.84.166.102	TCP	1314	[TCP segment of a reassembled PDU]
3502	-165.343592	10.92.32.10	10.84.166.102	TCP	1314	[TCP segment of a reassembled PDU]
3503	-165.343534	10.84.166.102	10.92.32.10	TCP	54	64806 → 80 [ACK] Seq=240 Ack=53754 Win=66560 Len=0
3504	-165.343490	10.92.32.10	10.84.166.102	TCP	1314	[TCP segment of a reassembled PDU]
3505	-165.343478	10.92.32.10	10.84.166.102	HTTP	1011	HTTP/1.1 200 OK (application/x-ns-proxy-autoconfig)
3506	-165.343457	10.84.166.102	10.92.32.10	TCP	54	64806 → 80 [ACK] Seq=240 Ack=55972 Win=66560 Len=0
3507	-165.343257	10.84.166.102	10.92.32.10	TCP	54	64806 → 80 [FIN, ACK] Seq=240 Ack=55972 Win=66560 Len=0
3509	-165.306572	10.92.32.10	10.84.166.102	TCP	60	80 → 64806 [ACK] Seq=55972 Ack=241 Win=15744 Len=0
3593	*REF*	10.84.166.102	10.86.35.73	TCP	1314	[TCP segment of a reassembled PDU]

```
[TCP Segment Len: 0]
Sequence number: 240    (relative sequence number)
Acknowledgment number: 55972    (relative ack number)
Header Length: 20 bytes
Flags: 0x011 (FIN, ACK)
```

Figure 6.7

And so, the TCP connection between the two devices will end.

2) UDP (User Datagram Protocol)

UDP is the exact opposite of TCP (it doesn't retransmit packets, doesn't establish a connection before sending data, doesn't establish the packets, etc.). **UDP simply sends** the **packets** from a specific **source** to a specific **destination** without being interested in the connection's status. The **advantage** of using this protocol is the **low latency**, which allows for the smooth transition of the application with the lowest delay possible.

Thus, UDP is **suitable** for **real-time applications** (e.g., Voice, Video traffic) that need to **reach** the **destination quickly**. In figure 6.8, you can see how the UDP header looks. Compared to TCP, it's much simpler and more efficient in processes and bandwidth utilization.

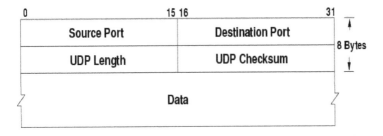

Figure 6.8

Because we were talking about real-time applications such as Skype, Facebook, CS Online, here are a few requirements for VoIP (**V**oice **o**ver **IP**) or other similar delay-sensitive apps:

- **Delay: < 150 ms:** Open CMD, type ping 8.8.8.8 and see the delay of every packet
- **Packet Loss: < 1%**: 1 second of voice = 50 packets of 20 ms audio each => 1% of 50 = 0,5; (this means that at every 2 seconds we can lose max 1 packet)
- **Jitter (variable delay): < 30ms**

At the beginning of this chapter, I told you that TCP uses segments (as the PDU), but things change a little bit in the case of the UDP protocol. **UDP** does not use segments and uses **datagrams** (it breaks the data into datagrams that are smaller in size than segments).

Figure 6.9 is an example of a UDP header (datagram). As you can see (compared to figure 6.2), it's much smaller than the TCP header (segment):

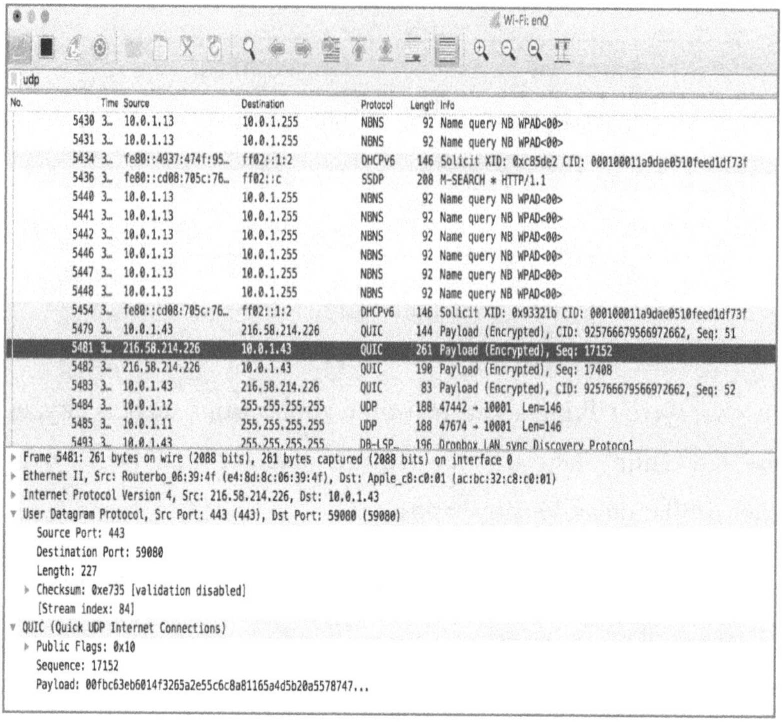

Figure 6.9

In figure 6.9, we can see the UDP protocol in action. This time I selected a protocol called QUIC (Quick UDP Internet Connections) that runs over UDP (as we can see in the figure). It helps with the **transmission of encrypted traffic** (the Payload is Encrypted).

I also want to state the reduced complexity of the UDP header (as seen in Figures 6.8 and 6.9), namely the **source port**, the **destination port** and the total length of the header.

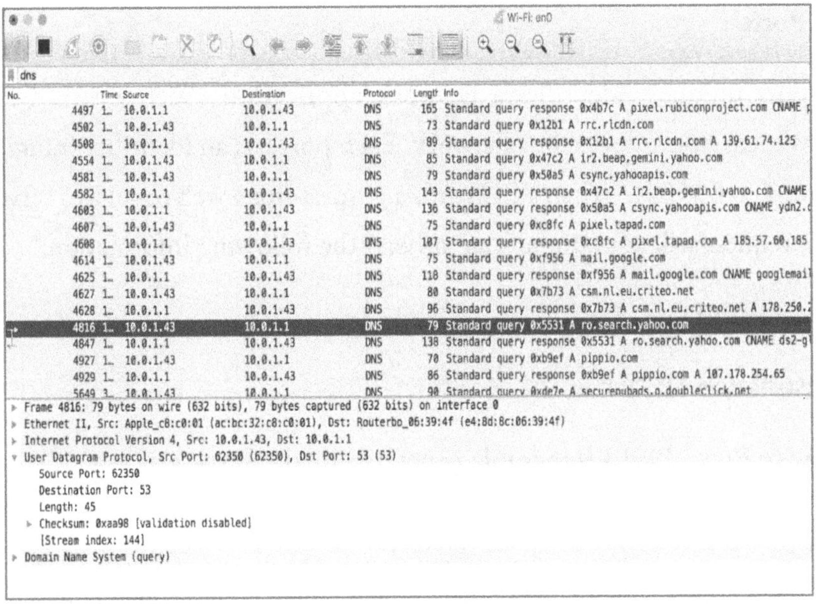

Figure 6.10

Now, let's take another example. In figure 6.10, we can see another type of traffic:

- **DNS queries** (name resolution of a domain to an IP address).
- We can see that the DNS protocol (which will be discussed in more detail in Chapter 7) uses UDP for data transportation, and to be more specific, it uses **port 53.** As you can see, I mentioned the term "port". In this case, we are not talking about a physical port (where you plug the cable in). Still, we refer to a **logical port**, which identifies the *network applications running* on a *device* (be it a Router, Server, Laptop, etc.).

3) Ports

A port uniquely identifies a **network application** (Web server, DNS server, etc.) on a device in a network. Each port has an identifier (ranging from **1** to **65535**). When a PC sends a request (for a web page) to a server, this request will contain (among others) the following information:

Source IP: PC

Destination IP: Server

Source Port: 29813 (randomly generated by the Browser)

Destination Port: 80

In other words: The PC's browser (with a source port of 29813) requests from the server (Destination) a web page (port 80).

Example #1 - TCP ports

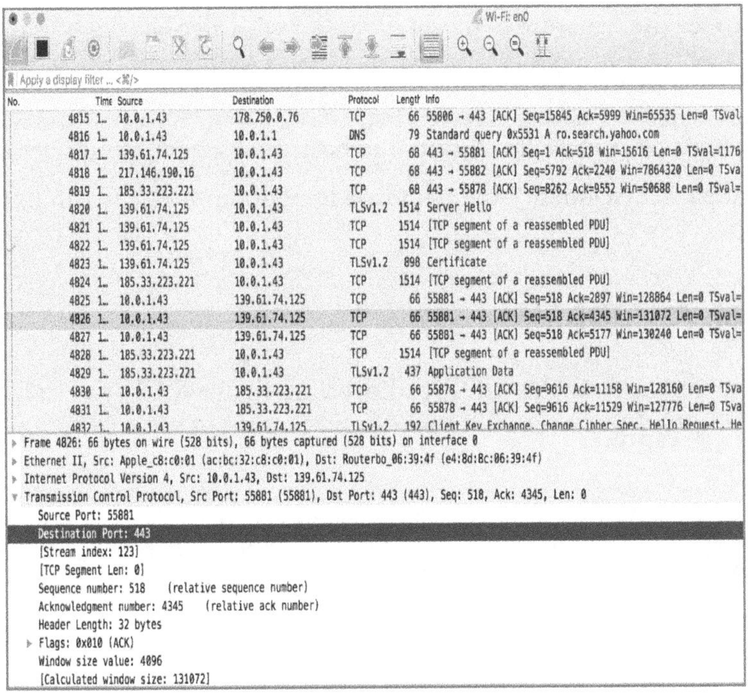

Figure 6.11

Now let's take a few examples where we can analyze and talk about what we've been discussing in this chapter.

As you can see in Figure 6.11, there is a communication flow between 2 devices (source: 10.0.1.43, destination: 139.61.74.125).

The **source port** (generated randomly) in this case is 55881 (most likely was generated by a browser - Google Chrome, Safari, Firefox, etc.), and the destination port is **443** (**HTTPS**, a secured web application).

Thus, the source addresses are requesting a web page hosted by a server placed somewhere on the Internet. Besides, in the lower half of the figure, you can see the structure of the TCP header with all of its fields that, have been shown in figure 6.1.

In this case, we can easily identify the ports, the sequence number of the current packet (segment), the acknowledgment number, the window size, etc.

Example #2 - UDP ports

Moving forward to the UDP protocol, in figure 6.12, you can see a Wireshark capture:

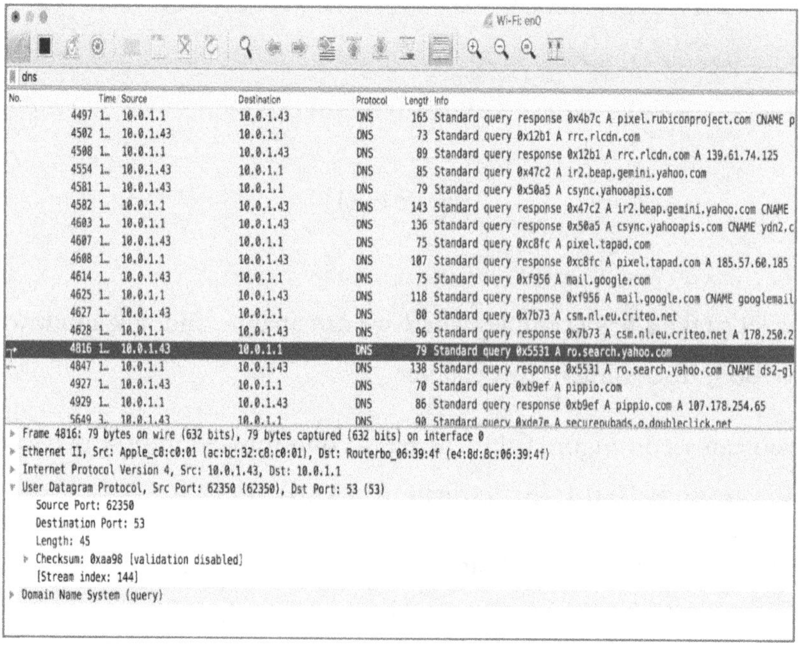

Figure 6.12

In the example from figure 6.12, you can see a process similar to the previous one, but in this case, it's the **UDP protocol** (actually DNS [layer 7], which uses the UDP protocol [layer 4]).

Here you can see the **two ports** (**source** - 62350 and **destination** - 53) of the two devices participating in the communication (source: 10.0.1.43 and destination: 10.0.1.1). I would like you to remember the simplicity of the UDP header (figure 6.12) versus the TCP header (figure 6.11). The most important elements in the UDP header are the two ports (source and destination).

Chapter 7

Layer 5, 6, 7 - Session, Presentation, Application

In this chapter, we will talk about the last three layers of the OSI model: **Session, Presentation** and **Application.** Let's get started with the first of the 3.

a) Layer 5 - Session

The purpose of the **Session Layer** is to *create, maintain, and terminate a session* between 2 network applications. A session (communication) consists of exchanging a request-to-answer data flow between 2 devices connected to the Internet. The device that **requests the data** is known as the **client**, while the device that **provides** the data is known as the **server**.

An important protocol at this layer is the Lightweight Directory Access Protocol (**LDAP**), a protocol that manages, searches and modifies a directory service (the place where the **user data** like *user names, passwords, and other user information,* is stored). With the help of this protocol, we can exchange user key elements in the network (more precisely, in the network security process):

- **User authentication**
- **User authorization**

b) Layer 6 - Presentation

The purpose of the presentation layer is to "serve data" in a specific format (e.g., JSON, JPEG image format, PNG, etc.). At this layer, **data is structured in a certain** form and is delivered to be interpreted by server-based applications.

For example, the data can be in one of the following formats: JSON (Figure 7.1), XML (Figure 7.2), etc.

```
{
    "employees": [
        {
            "id": 52626,
            "name": "Employee One"
        },
        {
            "id": 26565,
            "name": "Employee Two"
        }
    ]
}
```

Figure 7.1

```
<SampleXML>
  <Colors>
    <Color1>White</Color1>
    <Color2>Blue</Color2>
    <Color3>Black</Color3>
    <Color4 Special="Light">Green</Color4>
    <Color5>Red</Color5>
  </Colors>
  <Fruits>
    <Fruits1>Apple</Fruits1>
    <Fruits2>Pineapple</Fruits2>
    <Fruits3>Grapes</Fruits3>
    <Fruits4>Melon</Fruits4>
  </Fruits>
</SampleXML>
```

Figure 7.2

Another example of this layer is **data encryption**. Encrypted data (aka. secured data) is intended to hide the original content in another format. In Figure 7.3, you can see a capture of the encrypted traffic in Wireshark.

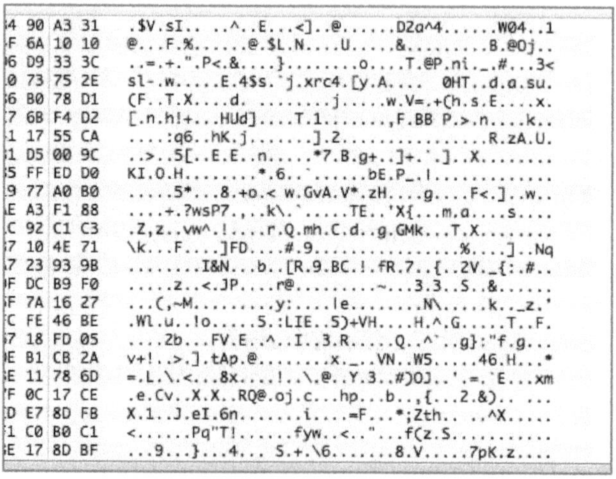

Figure 7.3

c) Layer 7 - Application

In this context, when talking about applications, we are strictly referring to **network applications**. These network applications are generally those offered by a server (e.g., a web application, email, remote access to a PC, etc.). Here are some protocols that work on this layer:

- **HTTPS** (port 443 TCP)
- **SSH** (port 22 TCP)
- **DHCP** (port 67/68 UDP)
- **DNS** (port 53 UDP)

For example, **HTTPS** (HyperText Transfer Protocol **Secure**) is a protocol that helps us with securely accessing websites. **HTTP** is the unsecured version that only offers the functionality (the ability to access web pages). Below in figure 7.4 is an example of the HTTPS protocol:

Figure 7.4

Another important protocol that helps us access the Internet (e.g., websites) is **DNS** (**D**omain **N**ame Services), which transforms a domain name (e.g., www.google.com) into an IP address (because all network devices **USE the addresses IP**, not the domain name).

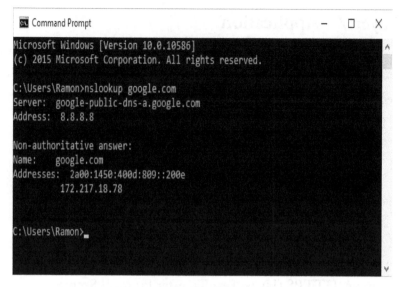

Figure 7.5

In figure 7.5, the IP address of Google.com is **172.217.18.78** and was found by using the **nslookup** command.

Network Applications

Now, let's take a look at a few of these applications. Below are a few protocols that are used very often by network applications:

HTTP

- **Description:** used for Web traffic (transports HTML files from a server to a client)
- **Port:** 80
- **Transport Protocol:** TCP

HTTPS

- **Description:** used for **securing** the Web traffic
- **Port:** 443
- **Transport Protocol:** TCP

FTP

- **Description:** allows the transfer of files between a client and a server
- **Port:** 20/21
- **Transport Protocol:** TCP

DNS

- **Description:** finds the IP address of a domain name (ex: google.com -> 172.217.18.67)
- **Port:** 53
- **Protocol de Transport:** UDP (client), TCP (server)

Telnet

- **Description:** remote access connection with a network device (Router, Switch, etc.) or server
- **Port:** 23
- **Transport Protocol:** TCP

SSH

- **Description: secured** remote access connection with a network device (Router, Switch) or server
- **Port:** 22
- **Transport Protocol:** TCP

DHCP

- **Description:** dynamically assigns IP addresses (and other info) to all end-device in the network
- **Port:** 67/68
- **Transport Protocol:** UDP

SMTP

- **Description:** mail transfer protocol, used between mail servers
- **Port:** 25
- **Transport Protocol:** TCP

IMAP

- **Description:** protocol for transferring mail from the server to the client (the emails will be stored on the server)
- **Port:** 143
- **Transport Protocol:** TCP

POP3

- **Description:** transfers emails from the server to the client (and stores them on the client's PC)
- **Port:** 110
- **Transport Protocol:** TCP

RDP

- **Description:** allows you to connect remotely (from the GUI) to a Windows, Linux, or macOS machine
- **Port:** 3389
- **Transport Protocol:** UDP

Now, let's take a more thorough look at some of the protocols mentioned above:

1) DHCP

DHCP (**D**ynamic **H**ost **C**onfiguration **P**rotocol) is a network protocol that dynamically provides the following information to the devices connected to the network:

1) IP Address + Mask

2) Default Gateway

3) DNS Server

The **IP address** will help us identify each device in the network, while the **network mask** establishes the network range (and size). The **DNS server** helps us **translate the name** (ex: google.com) into an **IP address** (216.58.214.227). All this information is provided by a server (in smaller networks, it's usually the Wireless Router).

How does DHCP work?

When an **end device** (PC, smartphone, tablet, smart TV, etc.) **connects** to the network, it will send a Broadcast request (to all network devices), hoping to **find a DHCP server** that can provide it with the information mentioned above. In figure 7.6, you can see the DHCP process happening between an end device and a DHCP server (Router in this scenario).

1) DHCP Discover

When a DHCP server (in small networks, it will generally be a Wi-Fi Router) sees such a message in the network, it will immediately respond with a:

2) DHCP Offer (which contains the information mentioned above)

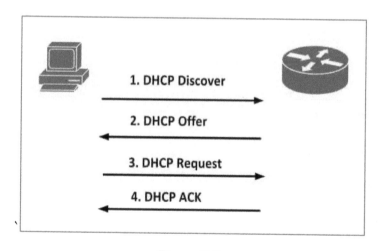

Figure 7.6

Finally, the device (the PC in this case) will agree to the DHCP server's "offer" and will send a request for it:

3) DHCP Request

After the DHCP server receives message #3, it will respond with:

4) DHCP ACK // as an acknowledgment of the request provided by the device

Configuring an IP address with DHCP on Windows

Now that you have seen how DNS works, let's take another example and see how we can assign an IP address via DHCP on Windows XP/7/8.1/10/11. We'll see how we can do this both from CMD and GUI.

1) Assigning an IP address with DHCP from the CMD

The way we can assign an IP address via DHCP in Windows from CMD is through the following command: **>ipconfig /renew**

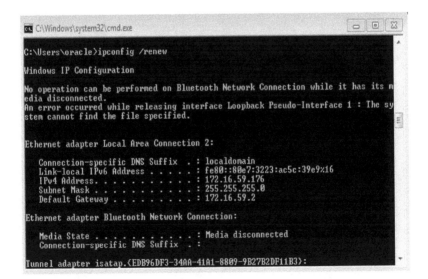

Figure 7.7

The result is an IP address, a subnet mask and a default gateway. If we want to find out more information (such as DNS, MAC address, or even DHCP server), we have the following command: **>ipconfig /all**

```
C:\Windows\system32\cmd.exe                                    □ ▣ ▨

   Primary Dns Suffix  . . . . . . . :
   Node Type . . . . . . . . . . . . : Hybrid
   IP Routing Enabled. . . . . . . . : No
   WINS Proxy Enabled. . . . . . . . : No
   DNS Suffix Search List. . . . . . : localdomain

Ethernet adapter Local Area Connection 2:

   Connection-specific DNS Suffix  . : localdomain
   Description . . . . . . . . . . . : Intel(R) PRO/1000 MT Network Connection #
2
   Physical Address. . . . . . . . . : 00-50-56-2B-12-94
   DHCP Enabled. . . . . . . . . . . : Yes
   Autoconfiguration Enabled . . . . : Yes
   Link-local IPv6 Address . . . . . : fe80::80e7:3223:ac5c:39e9%16(Preferred)
   IPv4 Address. . . . . . . . . . . : 172.16.59.176(Preferred)
   Subnet Mask . . . . . . . . . . . : 255.255.255.0
   Lease Obtained. . . . . . . . . . : Monday, August 14, 2017 12:11:21 PM
   Lease Expires . . . . . . . . . . : Monday, August 14, 2017 12:47:34 PM
   Default Gateway . . . . . . . . . : 172.16.59.2
   DHCP Server . . . . . . . . . . . : 172.16.59.254
   DHCPv6 IAID . . . . . . . . . . . : 352324649
   DHCPv6 Client DUID. . . . . . . . : 00-01-00-01-1D-C2-0B-B2-00-0C-29-98-5C-60

   DNS Servers . . . . . . . . . . . : 172.16.59.2
```

Figure 7.8

2) DHCP from the GUI in Windows

At this point, we can set up an IP address:

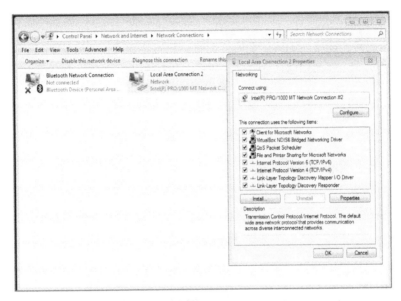

Figure 7.9

We'll select IPv4 -> "**Properties**" and get to the step from figure 7.10:

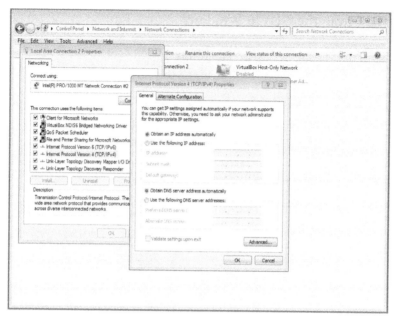

Figure 7.10

Now we'll select "**Obtain an IP address automatically**", followed by "**Obtain DNS server address automatically,**" and then press "**OK**". These two options will tell the PC to send a DHCP request on the network, requesting an IP address (+ the other settings).

2) Telnet

Telnet is a network protocol that allows remote connection to a network device (Router, Switch, Firewall, etc.) or a server. It is very widespread, being installed on the majority of devices. But it has a **major disadvantage**:

the connection is **UNSECURED**! All the communications between 2 devices using Telnet are sent in **clear text** and can be easily intercepted by a hacker.

A program we can use on Windows to achieve connectivity is PuTTY (http://www.putty.org/) (figure 7.11). With PuTTY, we can connect to a device via Telnet, SSH, or even through the console (Serial) via a cable.

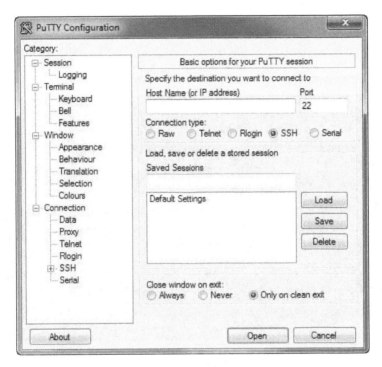

Figure 7.11

Telnet uses **port 23 on TCP** and can be used on Linux, Mac, Windows, or other devices. The recommendation is not to use it (because the **traffic is not encrypted**, only transmitted in clear text).

3) Secure Shell (SSH)

SSH is a protocol that **allows remote connections** to network devices (Router, Switch, Firewall, etc.) or servers (i.e., Linux, Unix, Windows). The **connection** is **SECURED** (both parties will encrypt all traffic).

This is **the most widely used** protocol for remote access due to its security and built-in flexibility.

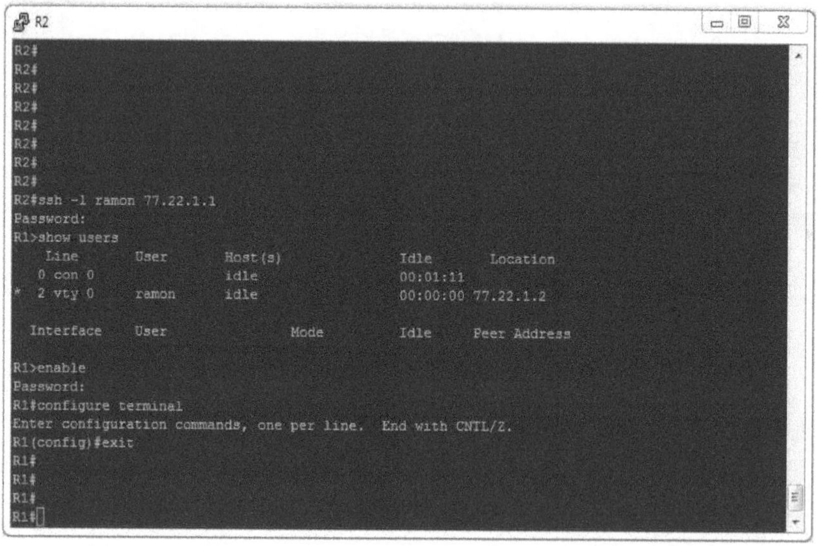

Figure 7.12

SSH uses **port 22 on TCP** and can be used on Linux, Mac, Windows, or other devices.

4) RDP - Remote Desktop Protocol

Because we spoke about two protocols that allow us to remotely access our network or our server devices (through the CLI), let's also look at a protocol that gives us the same capabilities of accessing a device remotely but comes with a graphical user interface (**GUI**). This protocol provides us access to our PC or laptop (Windows).

Here's an example of the RDP protocol, a scenario in which I connected (remotely through the Internet) to my desktop from another location.

Basically (in Windows), we have a window (Figure 7.13) with multiple fields in which we enter the IP address (or the name) of the PC, followed by the login credentials (user + password):

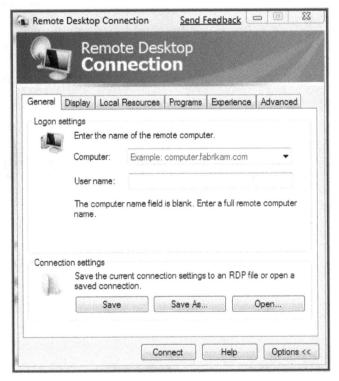

Figure 7.13

And in Figure 7.14, we can see what such an RDP connection looks like (a simple window where we have the desktop of the computer specified earlier).

Figure 7.14

Chapter 8

Cisco IOS & Intro to the CLI

When it comes to Cisco devices (Routers and Switches), they all have one thing in common: the **Cisco IOS**. **IOS** stands for the Internetwork **O**perating **S**ystem and is the "engine" that powers these network devices.

In the following chapter, we'll talk mainly about IOS and how we can manage it, but for now, I just want to let you know that we have two ways of working with it via the CLI or the GUI.

The **CLI** stands for the **C**ommand **L**ine **I**nterface and is the way we **configure** all **IOS** devices (we give special commands - from an interface-that will drive a certain behaviour). Thus, we will have **total control and access** to the Routers or Switches.

The **GUI** is the **G**raphical **U**ser **I**nterface and is a much friendlier way of managing a device. We often use it when setting up small network devices such as Home Wireless Routers (Wi-Fi).

The following section will see how we can interact with the Cisco IOS (versions **15.2** or **12.4**) through the CLI.

Introduction to the CLI - Basic Router Configurations

This section will move to the practical part of this eBook, and we'll start with the **basic configurations** of a Cisco Router. Also, here, we are going to use a network simulator (to create our network environments), so I highly recommend you download the **Cisco Packet Tracer** version **6.2** (which you can find **HERE (https://bit.ly/PKT-Cisco)**. This program gives us the ability to learn and practice the configuration of networks (PCs, network devices, servers, etc.) without requiring physical devices.

Here are some of the basic configurations that we're going to do on our Cisco Router:

- The **name** of the device (Hostname)
- **Passwords** (encrypted or in clear text)
- **IP addresses** on the interfaces
- **Remote access** on the network devices via Telnet or SSH

a) Access Levels

In Cisco IOS, we have **three** main **access levels** (for security purposes), where the user can do various things: #1 test the connectivity (to the Internet) (**>**) by using commands such as **ping** or **traceroute**; #2 **see** what's happening with the device (**#**); #3 make any **changes** - **(config)#**.

When you connect to a Cisco device (Router, Switch, Firewall, etc.), you will be in the **user exec mode (>)** - *1st access level*. In this access level (**user exec**), you are **limited** in the commands you can give to the device (generally commands such as ping, traceroute, etc.). To move up the ladder and access a higher level of commands and privileges, we must enter the following command:

Router>**enable**

We are officially in the 2nd access level, the **privilege mode - R1#**.

Here you can see configuration on the equipment (through various *show* commands), but you **CAN NOT make changes**.

Router>**enable**

Router#

To make changes to the device, we must go to a higher (the 3rd and last) access level, with even more privileges and known as the **global configuration mode**:

Router#**configure terminal**

Router(**config**)#

Here, you can make **any changes** you want to the device. The **global configuration mode** is equivalent to the Windows **Administrator** or the **root** user on Linux. Here are a few of the commands that I recommend you get familiar with:

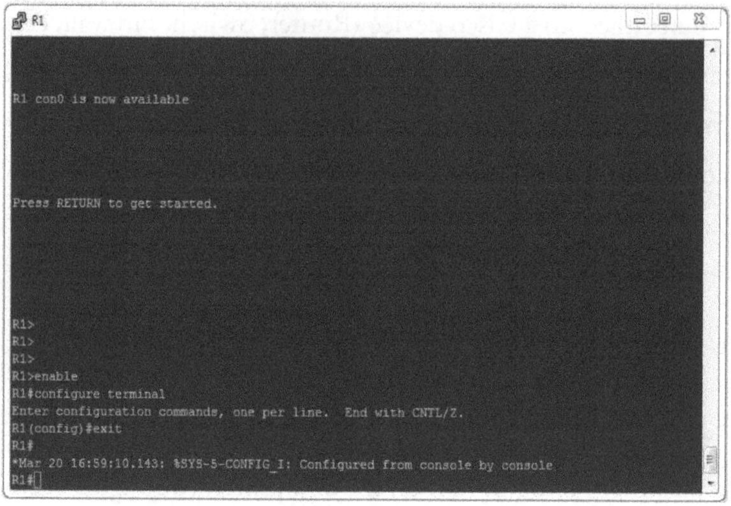

Figure 8.1

If we want to write a longer command (when not feeling like typing :D), we have a solution that provides us with a faster (and more accurate) way of inserting commands.

If I write the **R1#show run** command and press the **TAB** key, it will **auto-complete** it. Also "**?**" Will show us the (next) commands available.

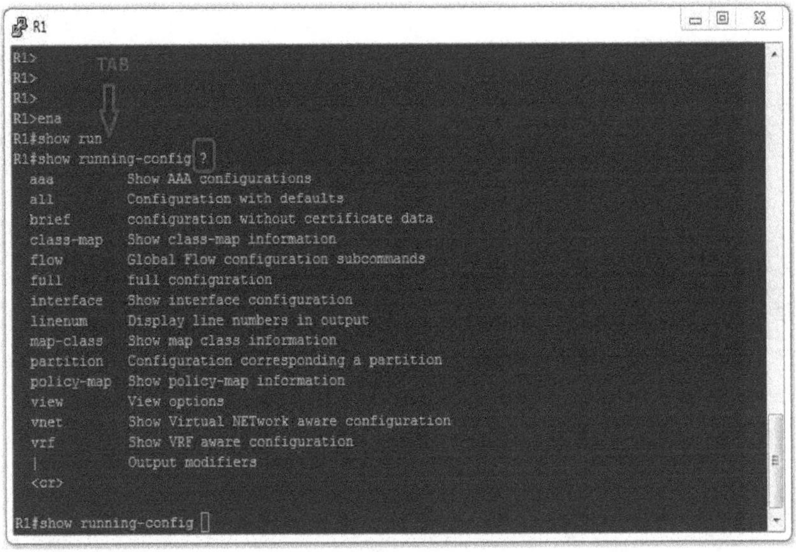

Figure 8.2

b) Setting a device name (Hostname)

To name the Router (or the Switch), we can enter the following command:

Router(config)#**hostname** *ROUTER_NAME*
ROUTER_NAME(config)#

Figure 8.3 illustrates this command and others from the following steps.

c) Securing access to the Router

Now, let's see how we can secure access to our Router by setting up a password. Here's how we can set up a **password** in **privilege mode (#)**:

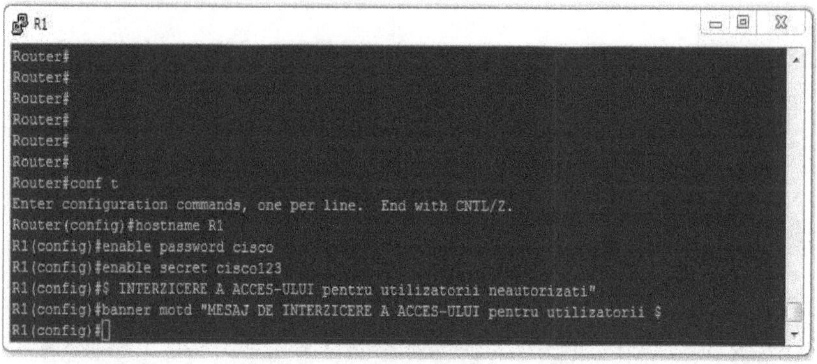

Figure 8.3

Router(config)#**hostname** R1

R1(config)#**enable password** cisco

or

R1(config)#**enable secret** cisco123

The following command will set a warning banner for those that try to login into the device:

R1(config)#**banner motd** "UNAUTHORISED ACCESS DENIED"

Maybe you're wondering about the difference between the *enable password* and the *enable secret* commands? Well, here's the difference (figure 8.4):

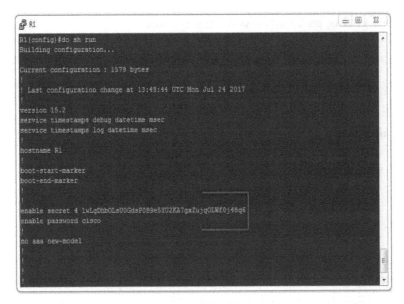

Figure 8.4

As you can see, one is stored in an **encrypted format** (#enable secret), and the other is stored in **clear tex**t (#enable password).

Let's take the following topology and start configuring the Router for network access (reachability):

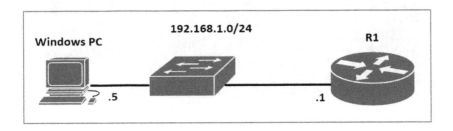

d) Configuring an IP address on the Router

As I said in Chapter 4, a Router **interconnects** multiple networks through **ports** (usually 2 or 3). We are calling **port** a physical place where a cable can be plugged. The other name that we assign to the logical part is an **interface**.

So, to sum things up:

- Port = Physical
- Interface = Logical

For example: "we will set an **IP** (logical) address on an **interface** and **connect** the cable (physically) to a **port**."

These interfaces must have an IP address configured to communicate within the network, and the interface must be turned **ON**. In figure 8.5, you can see how we can set an IP address on an interface:

```
R1

R1#
R1#
R1#
R1#conf t
Enter configuration commands, one per line.  End with CNTL/Z.
R1(config)#interface Gi3/0
R1(config-if)#ip address 192.168.1.1 255.255.255.0
R1(config-if)#no shutdown
R1(config-if)#
*Jul 24 13:47:46.979: %LINK-3-UPDOWN: Interface GigabitEthernet3/0, changed state to up
*Jul 24 13:47:47.979: %LINEPROTO-5-UPDOWN: Line protocol on Interface GigabitEthernet3/0, cha
nged state to up
```

Figure 8.5

R1(config)#**interface** FastEthernet0/0
R1(config-if)#**ip address** 192.168.1.1 255.255.255.0

R1(config-if)#**no shutdown**

f) Configuring remote access on a Router (Telnet, SSH)

A little earlier in chapter 7, we learned about Telnet and SSH, and now it's time to configure them on our Router. So let's move on first with Telnet:

Telnet

```
R1(config)#
R1(config)#
R1(config)#
R1(config)#
R1(config)#
R1(config)#
R1(config)#
R1(config)#
R1(config)#
R1(config)#
R1(config)#line vty 0 14
R1(config-line)#password cisco
R1(config-line)#login
R1(config-line)#exit
R1(config)#
```

Figure 8.6

R1(config)#**line vty** 0 14
R1(config-line)#**password** cisco
R1(config-line)#**login**

At first, we want to enter our **virtual lines** (15 in total), then set the password (in this case, "Cisco") and, in the end, start the Telnet process #login.

SSH

As we discussed in chapter 7, SSH is a protocol that ensures remote connection to a LAN or Internet device in a secure way. To **configure SSH on a Cisco device,** we have to take the following steps:

1. Creating a user and password
2. Setting a Domain name
3. Generating a pair of public & private keys - for security purposes
4. Enabling the process on the virtual lines (vty) with the command #login local

So, here (in figure 8.7) is the actual config of SSH on a Cisco Router:

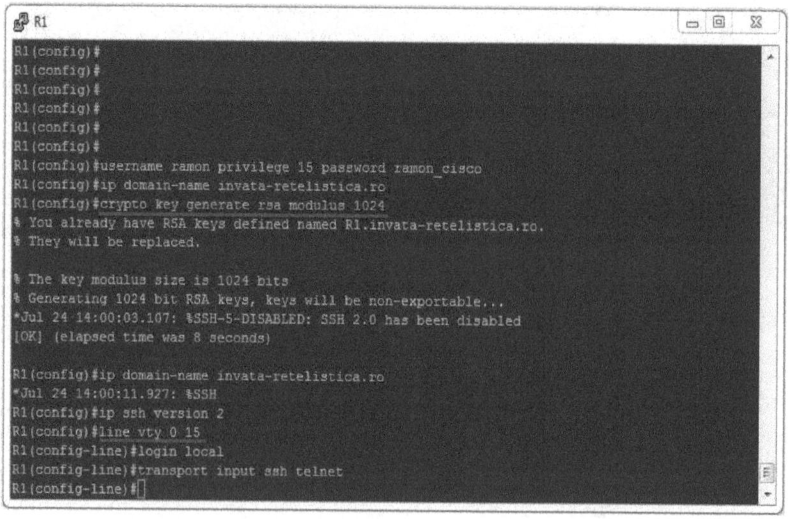

Figure 8.7

R1(config)#**username** admin **privilege** 15 **password** admincisco321

R1(config)#**ip domain-name** my.home.lab
R1(config)#**crypto key generate rsa modulus** 1024
R1(config)#**ip ssh version** 2

R1(config)**line vty** 0 15
R1(config-line)#**login local**
R1(config-line)#**transport input ssh telnet**

LAB #1

Now it's time to put theory into practice. In this lab, we are going to implement the concepts discussed above. Please follow the requirements below and configure the devices accordingly.

PURPOSE: Accommodation with the CLI. Basic configurations on Cisco Routers and Switches. Ensuring end-to-end connectivity

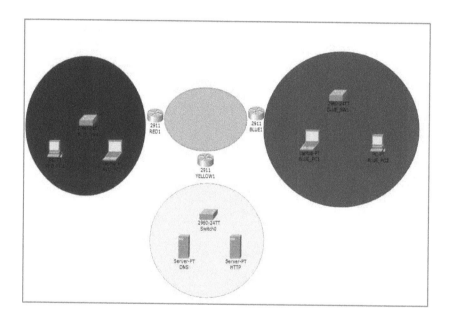

Lab Requirements

0) Wire the equipment properly (pay attention to the types of cables needed)

1) Set IP addresses on Routers, Switches, and PCs

- **RED**: (LEFT) 10.16.22.0/24

- **GREEN**: (MID) 89.12.0.0/24 (subnet this network into smaller ones of sizes no larger than 2 usable addresses)
- **BLUE**: (RIGHT) 192.168.0.64/27
- **YELLOW**: (DOWN) 172.30.33.128/25

Assign the first IP address of the network to the Routers, the following available IP addresses to the PCs, and the last IP address to the Switches.

2.1) Set the Hostname and enable password

2.2) Set the following Banners on the Routers:
("ONLY AUTHORIZED ACCESS")

3.1) Configure Telnet on RED1, RED_SW1, BLUE_SW1

- Use the password: secretP@$$

3.2) Configure SSH on BLUE1 and YELLOW1

- Use any username or password you like

4) Ensure end-to-end connectivity between the networks (by using Static Routes)

5) Test the connectivity with the ping command between:

- PCs within the same network (LAN - RED, BLUE)
- PCs & Routers
- PCs from opposite networks
- PCs and Servers (access their IP addresses from the built-in browser

Chapter 9

Basic Routing Concepts

1) How does a Router work?

First of all, let's recap, what is a Router? There is nothing more than a computer. It has the same features as this:

- Processor - **CPU**
- Memory **RAM** (128MB+ depends on the model), ROM
- Storage space in **Flash** - 32MB+ depends on the model
- **Operating system** - Cisco IOS

These hardware components propel the brain of each network equipment (Router, Switch, Firewall, etc.), namely the Cisco - IOS Operating System (OS). IOS comes from the Internetwork Operating System. This OS offers the "power" of the Router and makes the difference between Cisco and other network brands.

Cisco, at the moment, is the world leader in network equipment. They offer various solutions such as Routing, Switching, Security (Firewalls, IPS, SpamFilters, etc.) to Voice, Video, Data Center, etc. We will focus on elements related to the Routing side.

The router incorporating the elements described above must go through a process to become operational and ready to do the job. This startup process (boot) looks like this:

1. POST (Power-On Self Test): Hardware component test (CPU, RAM, etc.)
2. Bootstrap: establishes the location of the OS (Network - TFTP or Flash)
3. Uploads OS image to RAM:
4. Loads the configuration file: startup-config

All networking devices have a configuration file (called startup-config) in which the device settings are saved. This **startup-config** is in a special memory called **NVRAM** (Non-volatile RAM). This memory is a small one (<64kB) and does not erase the content when the stream is being taken (the Router stops or restarts).

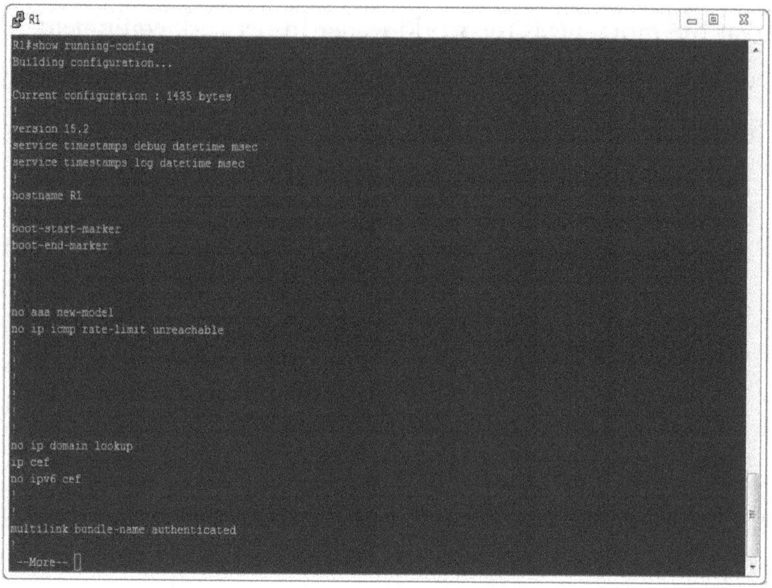

Figure 9.1

Once the machine is started, this startup-config is copied to RAM in a current configuration file called running-config. This file will contain the initial settings and those we added while the machine was working.

Any changes we make are written in **running-config**. Once we have saved the changes, they will be written in the startup-config!

If we do not save changes, they will be lost when the device is shut down (power loss, restart, etc.).

2) The Routing table

What is this routing table? It is where a Router stores information about different networks. It is the foundation that this network equipment uses.

Without its existence, the routing process (sending packets from one network to another). A routing table looks like this (see #show ip route (or #sh ip ro)):

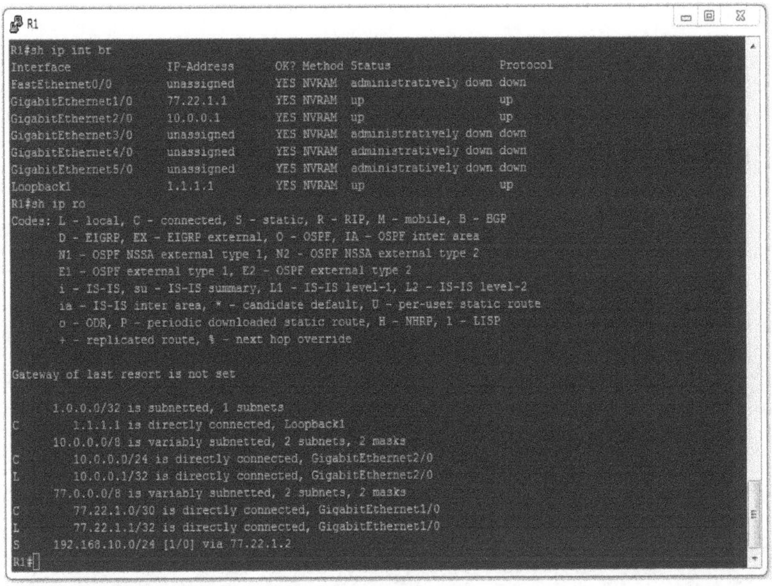

Figure 9.2

How does the routing work?

The purpose of a Router is to route packages. Instead, it has to make a logical decision (based on the routing table) on which interface to send the packet.

"The router receives traffic on an interface and must decide which interface it will send"

Route types

There are several types of routes:

- Directly connected - **C**
- Static - **S**
- Dynamic routing protocols - RIP (**R**), OSPF (**O**), EIGRP (**D**), BGP (**B**)

At first (after it started), a Router only knows of directly connected networks. These will appear in the routing table (#show ip route) with the letter C in front (as shown in the figure below). Letter L comes from Local and represents the IP address of a Router interface.

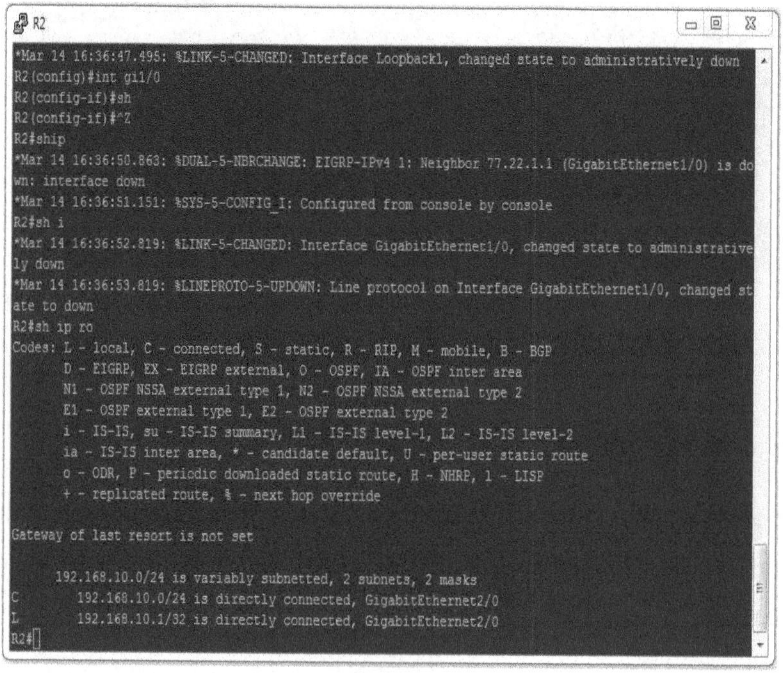

Figure 9.3

As you can see, the network directly connected is 192.168.10.0/24 and is located on the GigabitEthernet 2/0 interface. The IP address of the Router on this interface is 192.168.10.1

Administrative and Metric distance

Think of the information you heard from a very close friend vs. a person you've just met on the street. Who do you trust more? Clearly, as a friend. In this scenario, there are two different sources of information (friendship and alienation). Your confidence level will be higher with a friend than with a stranger.

A Router works in the same way when it comes to the source of information. This concept is called Administrative Distance (**AD**) and is a value between 0-255. A lower AD will always mean a higher confidence level in that route.

"**AD** = the most credible source."
"**Metric** = the best way to the destination. "

Each route type has such an AD. Example:

Route type	C (Connected)	S (Static)	D (EIGRP)	O (OSPF)	R (RIP)
AD	0	1	90	110	120

The metric is the factor (number) that determines the best route to the destination (which originates from the same source - e.g., OSPF).

For example, Google Maps can give you more suggestions to get from a specific source (e.g., Manchester, UK) to a specific destination (e.g., London, UK). You can reach London through Birmingham or Leicester, but which will be the fastest way? Well, here comes the metric, which can be: the fastest way or the shortest path.

Similarly, a routing protocol (OSPF, RIP, etc.) works, determining the shortest route to a particular destination (e.g., Google.com). It can choose the shortest path (based on the number of Routers or Bumpers) as the fastest way (link speeds).

Next-Hop and Output Interface - recursive routing

If we simplify things a lot, the Router has to do one thing: get a packet on an interface (process it) and send it to another interface.

It connects with other networks (thus forming the Internet). To send a packet from a source to a destination, the Router needs to know the CUI must send it (or, more precisely, which interface). Suppose we have the following network topology:

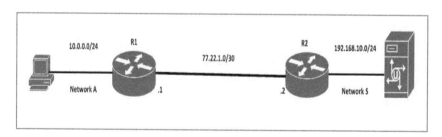

Figure 9.4

We want to send a message from the Network A PC (IP: 10.0.0.9) to the S-Server (IP: 192.168.10.11). When the message arrives at R1, it has to decide (more specifically, it must decide who will send that message so that it arrives at the destination (Server Network)).

R1 looks at his routing table and asks if he has a route to the 192.168.10.0/24 network. R1 will forward the message (to R2) if this route exists. Otherwise, the message will be discarded if the route does not exist.

When the message reaches R2, it will forward it (to the destination).

Chapter 10

Static Routes

Throughout this chapter, we will discuss the Static Routes, namely: Why do we need them, their advantages and disadvantages and how to configure them. To begin with, we'll use the topology below to understand the concept:

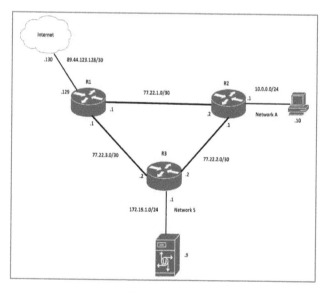

Figure 10.1

Why do we need Static Routes?

By default, a Router only knows Direct Connected networks. He does not know how to send these packets further. This is where we, those who manage these devices and configure the routes on the device.

When a Router starts, it first learns the directly connected networks (those starting with C in the table below).

In the figure below, you can see the routing table of a Cisco Router that contains the routers/networks directly connected (C) and the R2 address of R2 on those interfaces (L).

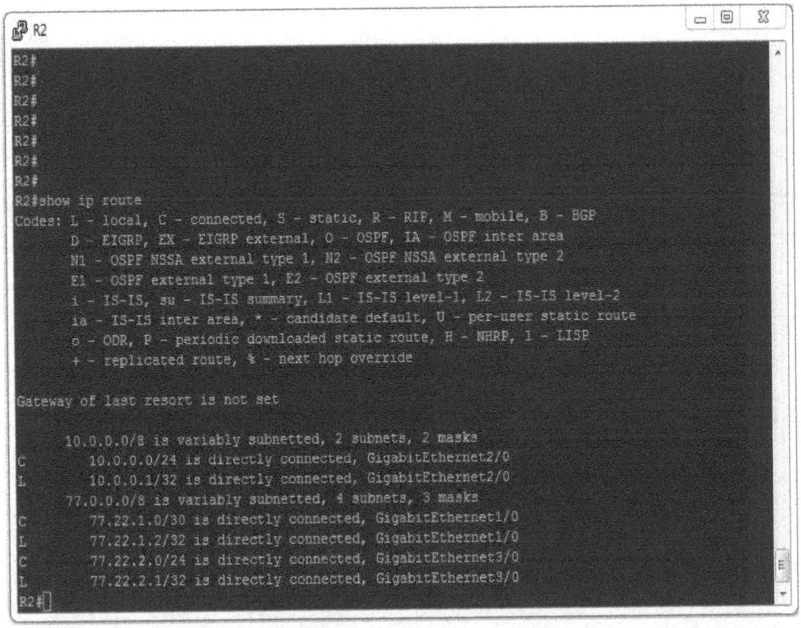

Figure 10.2

The Router does not know how to send traffic (further away from directly connected networks). This is where we, those who manage these devices and configure the routes on the device.

There are two ways we can tell a Router how it can reach a particular network (destination):

1. **Manual** - using Static Routes
2. **Dynamic** - Routers communicate with each other and set the best (fast) route to a network (destination)

Static routes are very important for network connectivity (or the Internet). When we enter a static route in the routing table, it will appear as follows:

```
R3#
R3#
R3#
R3#
R3#show ip route
Codes: L - local, C - connected, S - static, R - RIP, M - mobile, B - BGP
       D - EIGRP, EX - EIGRP external, O - OSPF, IA - OSPF inter area
       N1 - OSPF NSSA external type 1, N2 - OSPF NSSA external type 2
       E1 - OSPF external type 1, E2 - OSPF external type 2
       i - IS-IS, su - IS-IS summary, L1 - IS-IS level-1, L2 - IS-IS level-2
       ia - IS-IS inter area, * - candidate default, U - per-user static route
       o - ODR, P - periodic downloaded static route, H - NHRP, l - LISP
       + - replicated route, % - next hop override

Gateway of last resort is not set

      10.0.0.0/24 is subnetted, 1 subnets
S        10.0.0.0 [1/0] via 77.22.2.1
      77.0.0.0/8 is variably subnetted, 4 subnets, 2 masks
C        77.22.2.0/24 is directly connected, GigabitEthernet2/0
L        77.22.2.2/32 is directly connected, GigabitEthernet2/0
C        77.22.3.0/24 is directly connected, GigabitEthernet1/0
L        77.22.3.2/32 is directly connected, GigabitEthernet1/0
      172.19.0.0/16 is variably subnetted, 2 subnets, 2 masks
C        172.19.1.0/24 is directly connected, GigabitEthernet3/0
L        172.19.1.1/32 is directly connected, GigabitEthernet3/0
R3#
```

Figure 10.3

In the routing table in the figure above, the static route is S 10.0.0.0 [1/0] via 77.22.2.1. Here is what these are:

- S represents the type of route (**Static**)
- 10.0.0.0/24 is the destination network
- [1/0] - **1** represents **AD** (Administrative Distance),and **0** represents **Metric**

Advantages / Disadvantages

There are two ways a Router can learn about a particular network:

- *Static Route*
- *Dynamic Routing Protocol* (we will see in Chapter 3)

Advantages of **Static Routes vs. Dynamic Protocols:**

- Manually set by an administrator (thus adding an extra level of security)
- They are suitable for small networks (more networks = more static routes).
- Do not consume resources (CPU, RAM)

Disadvantages of **Static Routes vs. Dynamic Protocols**

- Does not automatically adapt to network changes (requires administrator intervention
- The configuration and management become complex with the growth of the network
- Configuration errors can easily occur

How do we configure Static Routes?

In this part, we will see how to set up static routes (to improve your knowledge with the help of the two laboratories at the end). Let's take the following scenario:

Let's assume that the PC in network A wants to access the services (Web, File Transfer, etc.) from the S network server, and we need to do that.

As I said at the beginning of this chapter, Routers, by default, do not know of networks other than those directly connected (in the case of R2 - network A, the network between R2 - R3, and in the case of R3 - network S, the network of R2 and R3). Thus, R2 knows how to reach R3 but does not know how to reach the S.

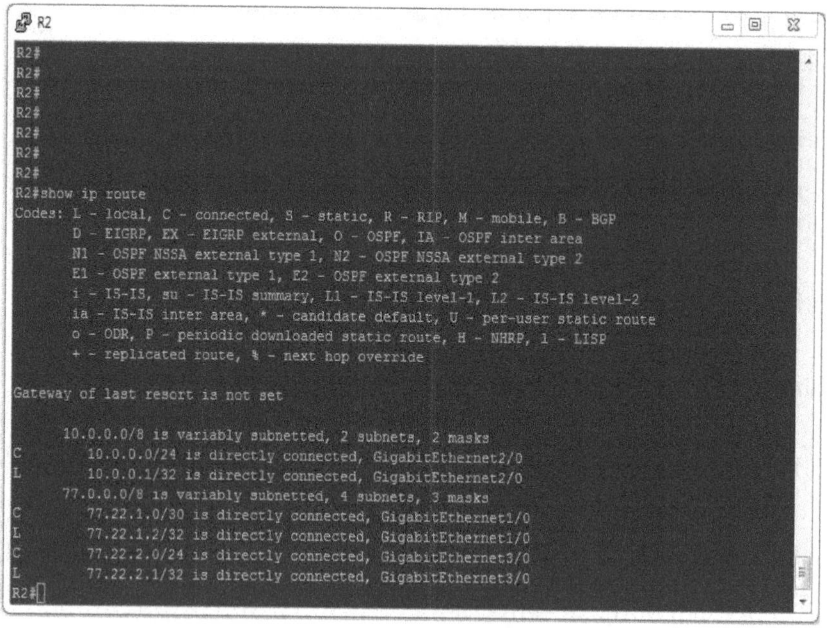

Figure 10.4

We will set a static route on R2 to the S network (172.19.1.0/24). This is not enough to send traffic between the two networks because:

1. R2 knows how to send traffic to the server
2. But return traffic (return from Server to PC) will block at R3 because it does not know how to get into network A (10.0.0.0/24).

Initial traffic: **A->R2->R3->S**

Return traffic: **S->R3->?** (Result => **Drop**)

To set a static route on R2 to network S (server) and R3 to network A, we will enter the following commands:

R2(config)#**ip route** 172.19.1.0 255.255.255.0 77.22.2.2

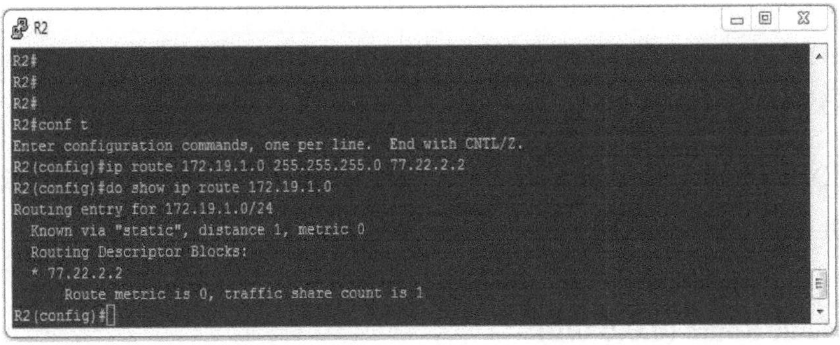

Figure 10.5

R3(config)#**ip route** 10.0.0.0 255.255.255.0 77.22.2.1

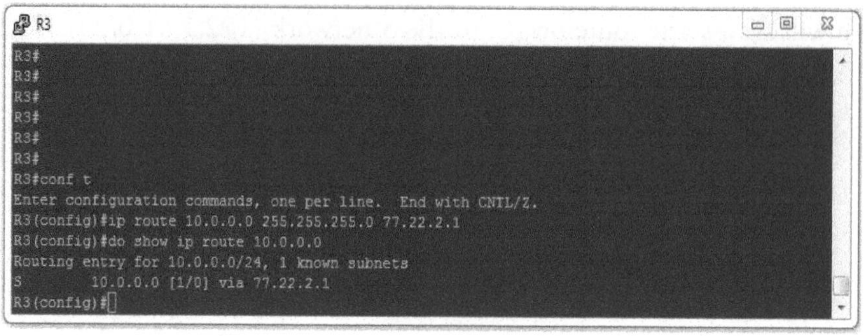

Figure 10.6

The structure of this command looks like this :

R1(config)#**ip route** DESTINATION_NETWORK MASK NEXT_HOP

DESTINATION_NETWORK = where I want to get (for R2, it will be 172.19.1.0/24 (S), and for R3 will be 10.0.0.0/24 (A)

MASK = network mask of destination network (for /24, it will be 255.255.255.0)

NEXT_HOP = Specifies who they reach the destination network. R2 will reach the S via R3

Default Route (0.0.0.0/0)

There is a special static route known as the **Default Route** (aka 0.0.0.0/0). The role of the default route is to tell the Router where to send all of the traffic (to a specific destination that the Router doesn't know about). This route is useful when we have a connection to the Internet through a single Router and we want to send all traffic (for the Internet) to this Router.

```
R1                                                                    ▭ ▣ ☒

Enter configuration commands, one per line.  End with CNTL/Z.
R1(config)#ip route 0.0.0.0 0.0.0.0 89.44.123.130
R1(config)#do show ip route
Codes: L - local, C - connected, S - static, R - RIP, M - mobile, B - BGP
       D - EIGRP, EX - EIGRP external, O - OSPF, IA - OSPF inter area
       N1 - OSPF NSSA external type 1, N2 - OSPF NSSA external type 2
       E1 - OSPF external type 1, E2 - OSPF external type 2
       i - IS-IS, su - IS-IS summary, L1 - IS-IS level-1, L2 - IS-IS level-2
       ia - IS-IS inter area, * - candidate default, U - per-user static route
       o - ODR, P - periodic downloaded static route, H - NHRP, l - LISP
       + - replicated route, % - next hop override

Gateway of last resort is 89.44.123.130 to network 0.0.0.0

S*    0.0.0.0/0 [1/0] via 89.44.123.130
      77.0.0.0/8 is variably subnetted, 4 subnets, 2 masks
C        77.22.1.0/30 is directly connected, GigabitEthernet1/0
L        77.22.1.1/32 is directly connected, GigabitEthernet1/0
C        77.22.3.0/30 is directly connected, GigabitEthernet3/0
L        77.22.3.1/32 is directly connected, GigabitEthernet3/0
      89.0.0.0/8 is variably subnetted, 2 subnets, 2 masks
C        89.44.123.0/24 is directly connected, GigabitEthernet2/0
L        89.44.123.129/32 is directly connected, GigabitEthernet2/0
R1(config)#
```

Figure 10.7

In the example above, R1 is connected to the Internet, and we set a static default (S *):

R1(config)#**ip route** 0.0.0.0 0.0.0.0 89.44.123.130

So if we want to get to google.com (or any other resource on the Internet), we can do that! We have to add default static routes to both R2 and R3 to R1 so that the PC and the server can access the Internet.

R2(config)#ip route 0.0.0.0 0.0.0.0 77.22.1.1

R3(config)#**ip route 0.0.0.0 0.0.0.0** 77.22.3.1

Checking the settings

To verify that everything is working properly, we have several commands available to help us check/test if what I have configured works. From R2, we give the following commands:

R2#**show ip route** //to see the routing table

R2#**ping** 89.44.123.129 //to see if we have access to the Internet

R2#**show run | section route** // to check the commands you entered earlier

```
R2                                                                    _ □ ☒

         o - ODR, P - periodic downloaded static route, H - NHRP, l - LISP
         + - replicated route, % - next hop override

Gateway of last resort is 77.22.1.1 to network 0.0.0.0

S*     0.0.0.0/0 [1/0] via 77.22.1.1
       10.0.0.0/8 is variably subnetted, 2 subnets, 2 masks
C          10.0.0.0/24 is directly connected, GigabitEthernet2/0
L          10.0.0.1/32 is directly connected, GigabitEthernet2/0
       77.0.0.0/8 is variably subnetted, 4 subnets, 3 masks
C          77.22.1.0/30 is directly connected, GigabitEthernet1/0
L          77.22.1.2/32 is directly connected, GigabitEthernet1/0
C          77.22.2.0/24 is directly connected, GigabitEthernet3/0
L          77.22.2.1/32 is directly connected, GigabitEthernet3/0
       172.19.0.0/24 is subnetted, 1 subnets
S          172.19.1.0 [1/0] via 77.22.2.2
R2#sh run | section route
ip route 0.0.0.0 0.0.0.0 77.22.1.1
ip route 172.19.1.0 255.255.255.0 77.22.2.2
R2#ping 89.44.123.129
Type escape sequence to abort.
Sending 5, 100-byte ICMP Echos to 89.44.123.129, timeout is 2 seconds:
!!!!!
Success rate is 100 percent (5/5), round-trip min/avg/max = 16/36/64 ms
R2#
```

Figure 10.8

LAB #2

Now I came to the laboratory part (the practical part), which you included in the attachments. Here we are going to implement the steps discussed above. Follow your existing lab requirements and configure the existing devices accordingly.

PURPOSE: Basic Configurations of Static Routes on Routers

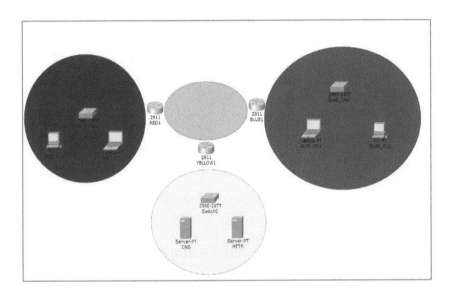

TIP: Use **this commands guide** (http://amzn.to/2pkG0Oq) to solve the exercise successfully!

You can download the labs from the following link. Click here (http://bit.ly/IT-Labs)

LAB #3

Now we are going to deepen the ones discussed above. Follow your existing lab requirements and configure the existing devices accordingly.

PURPOSE: Streamline Static Routing knowledge on a larger network

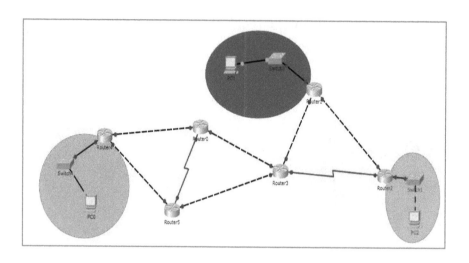

TIP: Use **this commands guide** (http://amzn.to/2pkG0Oq) to solve the exercise successfully!

You can download the labs from the following link. Click here (http://bit.ly/IT-Labs)

Chapter 11

Routing Protocols

Distance Vector vs. Link State

When talking about dynamic routing protocols, we generally refer to 2 classes:

- Distance Vector (RIP, EIGRP)
- Link State (OSPF, IS-IS)

Distance Vector is those routing protocols based on the "**Routing by rumor**" principle (I'm basing on the information I received from my neighbor, I do not have an overview of the entire network). This category includes protocols such as RIP and EIGRP (considered a hybrid protocol).

Link State are those routing protocols that have an overview (an **exact map**) of the entire network. I know "everything moves". They have information about each link (its current status: up / down, the speed of that link - 100Mbps, 1Gbps, etc.). This includes OSPF and IS-IS protocols.

Distance Vector

RIP (Routing Information Protocol)

What is RIP?

Practically at the beginning (once the boot/boot process has finished), each Router only knows the directly connected networks. Once we start RIP on them, each Router, in part, will tell the neighbor about its directly connected routes. So each Router will learn at least one neighbor's route. At this point, the equipment stores all this information in a Table - Route Table.

Each Router, in part, will send all the information you know about the network (aka Route Table) to its directly connected neighbors. The process is repeated until each RIP "running" device knows how to reach each point of the network.

This routing table submission process (RIP Updates) is a repetitive one and takes place every 30 seconds (Update Timer). So within a time frame, each Router will know each network individually.

How does RIP work?

RIP establishes the shortest path to a network destination based on the metric. In this case, the metric is the number of hops (more exactly, how many routers do I need to get to reach the destination?)

RIP also has certain **disadvantages,** such as:

- A network can be up to 15 hops away
- Automatically summarizes networks (there is a risk that Routers will not learn all networks)
- Rare updates (at every **30 seconds**)
- A 20 seconds network downtime may involve financial damage

Take the example below (used earlier):

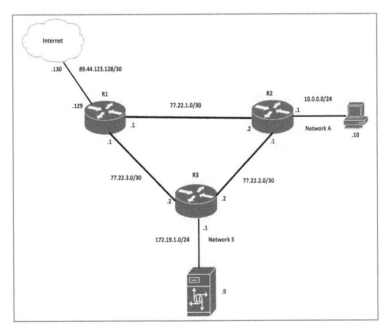

Figure 11.1

If we want to send traffic from PC to Server, the Router has two possibilities:

1. Sends R3's traffic to the Server
   a. PC -> R2 -> R3 -> Server **(2 Hops)**
2. Sends R1's traffic, which is forwarded to R3, which sends to the Server
   b. PC -> R2 -> R1 -> R3 -> Server **(3 Hops)**

The shortest way, in this case, is the first. So R2 will install in its Routing Table:

172.19.1.0/24 [120/2] via 77.22.2.2 (R3's IP), where 120 represents AD and 2 represents the metric.

RIP has two versions, v1 is not used anymore, and the current version, v2, is the one used (only when applicable, i.e., when RIP is used). As I said before, RIP is an old routing protocol and quite low in terms of features, so it is no longer used (except in some cases).

In different books or networking courses, the purpose of the RIP is a didactic one because it illustrates very well how a routing protocol works (so switching from RIP to OSPF or EIGRP is easier).

Configuring RIP on Cisco Routers

Now let's see how we can configure RIP on a Cisco Router. Here are the commands:

On R2:

R2(config)#**router rip**

R2(config-router)#**version 2**

R2(config-router)#**no auto-summary**

R2(config-router)#**network** 77.22.2.0

R2(config-router)#**network** 77.22.1.0

R2(config-router)#**network** 10.0.0.0

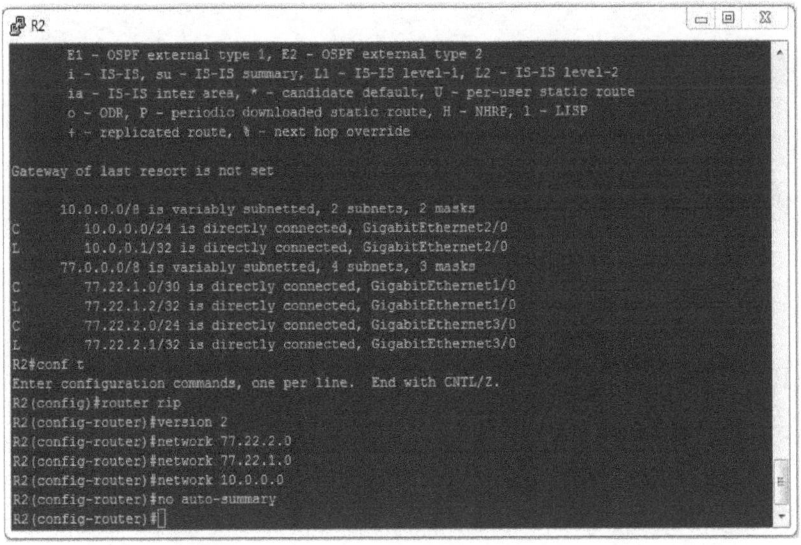

Figure 11.2

On R3:

R3(config)#**router rip**

R3(config-router)#**version 2**

R3(config-router)#**no auto-summary**

R3(config-router)#**network** 77.22.2.0

R3(config-router)#**network** 77.22.3.0

R3(config-router)#**network** 172.19.1.0

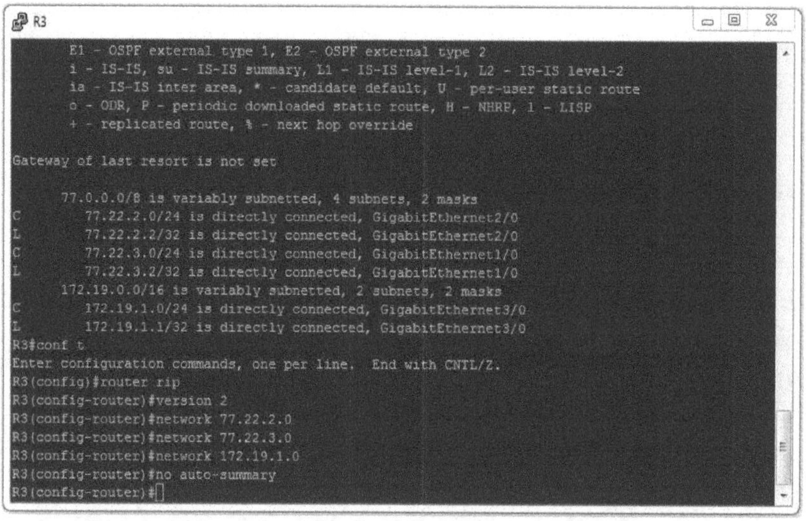

Figure 11.3

On R1:

R1(config)#**ip route** 0.0.0.0 0.0.0.0 89.44.123.130

R1(config)#router rip

R1(config-router)#version 2

R1(config-router)#no auto-summary

R1(config-router)#network 77.22.3.0

R1(config-router)#network 77.22.1.0

R1(config-router)#default-information originate

```
R1#
R1#conf t
Enter configuration commands, one per line.  End with CNTL/Z.
R1(config)#ip route 0.0.0.0 0.0.0.0 89.44.123.130
R1(config)#router rip
R1(config-router)#version 2
R1(config-router)#network 77.22.1.0
R1(config-router)#network 77.22.3.0
R1(config-router)#default-information originate
R1(config-router)#
```

Figure 11.4

We start the RIP process by the command: rip router, then set its version (2). The #no auto-summary command is required for RIP not to summarize the networks automatically. A summarization of networks may lead to the miss exchange of information. Thus end-to-end connectivity is being compromised.

By command #network, we specify which networks we want to send to the other Routers and which interfaces these Updates will be sent to. The # default-information command originated will propagate the default route (ip route 0.0.0.0) to the other Routers.

Checking the configurations

Once we've made the settings, it's important to check (and understand) what we have done so far. In the figure below, you can see how on R2, I used the #show ip route command to check the routing table (where you can see dynamically learned networks written with R).

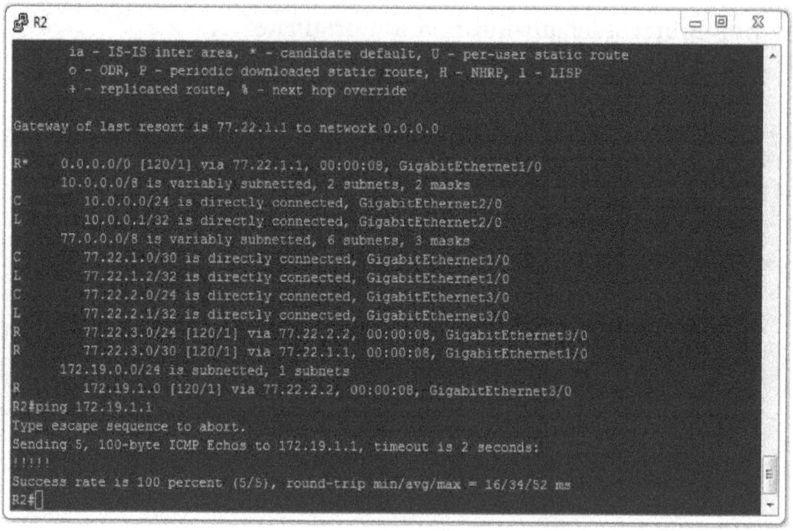

Figure 11.5

The following command I used is #ping 172.19.1.1, with which we tested connectivity to a dynamically learned route.

Another extremely useful command is #show ip protocols to help you learn more about your router routing protocols.

In figure 3.6 below, you can see:

- The routing Protocol is **RIP and uses** version **2**
- Routing is started on the 3 Gigabit Ethernet interfaces
- Summarized networks for which **network command was given**
- Administrative Distance (**AD**) of the RIP- **120**
- Protocol timers (30s - Updates, 180s hold down timer)

```
R2#show ip protocols
*** IP Routing is NSF aware ***

Routing Protocol is "rip"
  Outgoing update filter list for all interfaces is not set
  Incoming update filter list for all interfaces is not set
  Sending updates every 30 seconds, next due in 24 seconds
  Invalid after 180 seconds, hold down 180, flushed after 240
  Redistributing: rip
  Default version control: send version 2, receive version 2
    Interface           Send Recv Triggered RIP Key-chain
    GigabitEthernet1/0    2    2
    GigabitEthernet2/0    2    2
    GigabitEthernet3/0    2    2
  Automatic network summarization is not in effect
  Maximum path: 4
  Routing for Networks:
    10.0.0.0
    77.0.0.0
  Routing Information Sources:
    Gateway         Distance      Last Update
    77.22.1.1         120         00:00:00
    77.22.2.2         120         00:00:04
  Distance: (default is 120)
```

Figure 11.6

So the recommended commands to check the settings are:

R2#show ip protocols

R2#show ip route

R2#show run | section rip

R2#[ping | traceroute] IP address

Route Selection Process from the Routing Table

When routers have to make the routing decision, they look for the best route to the destination in the routing table. The router will go through the routing table based on algorithms that try to reduce search time. But at one point, this happened:

IP Destination: 172.16.0.10

And the Router has three different networks available:

172.16.0.0/16 via GigabitEthernet **0/1**
172.16.0.0/18 via GigabitEthernet **0/2**
172.16.0.0/26 via GigabitEthernet **0/3**

The Router has to decide which of these will be the destination network to know which interface to send the packet. The router will do Longest Match Routing, meaning it will take the largest mask (with most network bits) and choose it as the destination network because it thinks the network is more specific.

Let's take the example below to understand better:

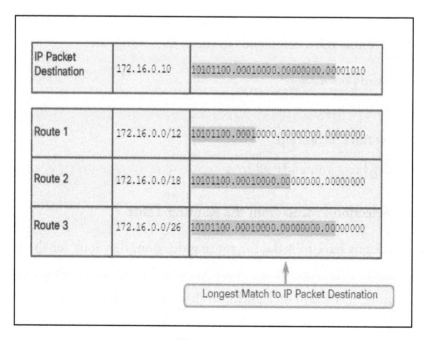

Figure 11.7

Thus the third route with the most common network bits (the largest mask) will be the way to the destination for the host 172.16.0.10

Conclusion

RIP is a protocol used for small networks (max. 15 hops distance). Today this protocol is no longer used (except in some situations), but it is very useful to understand how Dynamic Routing works. Also, I learned that Routers (when they have a decision to make) choose the most specific mask when there are more possibilities for a destination.

LAB #4

Now I came to the laboratory part (the practical part), which you included in the attachments. Here we are going to implement the ones discussed above. Follow your existing lab requirements and configure the existing devices accordingly.

PURPOSE: Basic configuration for RIP

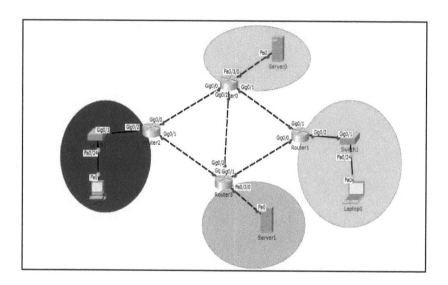

TIP: Use **this commands guide** (http://amzn.to/2pkG0Oq) to solve the exercise successfully!

You can download the labs from the following link. Click here (http://bit.ly/IT-Labs)

LAB #5

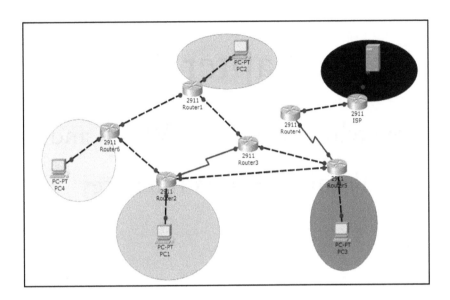

Now I came to the laboratory part (the practical part), which you included in the attachments. Here we are going to implement the ones discussed above. Follow your existing lab requirements and configure the existing devices accordingly.

PURPOSE: Practice the use of routing protocols (RIP)

TIP: Use **this commands guide** (http://amzn.to/2pkG0Oq) to solve the exercise successfully!

You can download the labs from the following link. Click here (http://bit.ly/IT-Labs)

Chapter 12

Switching Concepts. VLAN and Trunk & Access Interfaces

Because in the previous chapters, we talked about Routers and the routing process (practically how the data is transmitted through the Internet), in this chapter, we'll talk in more detail about Switches. We'll see what the VLAN concept represents and what Trunk and Access interfaces are. Trunk and Access are used by most of the medium and large networks.

1) VLAN (Virtual Local Area Network)

VLAN means **Virtual LAN** (Local Area Network) and has the purpose of separating (in a virtual way) the networks that are connected to the same physical equipment (Switch). **VLAN**s allow us to separate (from a logical point of view) more devices (PCs, Laptops) connected to the same Switch. In short words, we can say this:

One VLAN = One Network = One Broadcast Domain

So, a VLAN represents a network. If we choose to create 2 VLANs, we will have two different networks (2 Broadcast domains as well).

VLANs are used everywhere in big companies. Allow me to present a few examples:

#Ex1: The Wireless Network **Guest** and **Internal**; come from the same Wireless Router, but they are logically separated. By default, you can't have access from the network Guest to the network Internal, and neither the other way around.

NOTE: This way, we obtain a logical separation, which logically takes to **segmentation** and an increase of the **security level** in the network.

#Ex2: in all the average and large companies, where a separation of the devices on departments is desired (for example, the IT department (ex: VLAN 45) will not be able to access all the resources in the Marketing department (ex: VLAN 91))

NOTE: to identify different departments, VLANs are using a unique ID (an identification number) that can be given a name (for easier identification).

So, the ID of a VLAN can fall into the next categories:

- **Standard** VLAN ID – 1 – 1005
- **Extended** VLAN ID – 1006 – 4094

As you can see, there is also an extended range of IDs that have been added afterward, after the standard for the VLANs has been created, the purpose of this range being to increase the total number of VLANs that can exist on a Switch, and also to allow the use of routing application on level 3 Switches.

Before we move forward, I also want to mention that VLAN is a standard in the industry, which has the name **IEEE 802.1q**. This makes the technology available on Cisco equipment and on Juniper, Huawei, HP, etc. This technology is an advantage, thanks to the existing interoperability between devices.

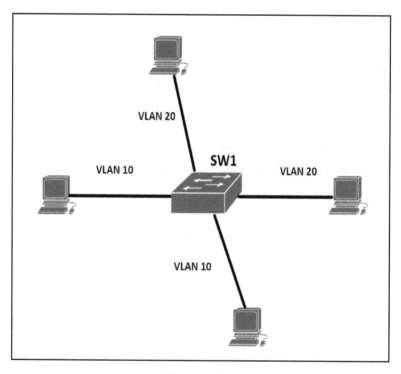

Figure 12.1

In figure 12.2, you have a clearer representation of the PCs that can communicate between them. So, as you can see, only the PCs in the same VLAN can communicate with each other.

All the equipment is physically connected to the same Switch, but they are being separated logically. Why? Because the Switch adds a tag specifying the fact that only the equipment with the same tag (aka. VLAN ID) can communicate in between them (in this scenario, only the PCs in the green circle, respectively the ones in the red circle).

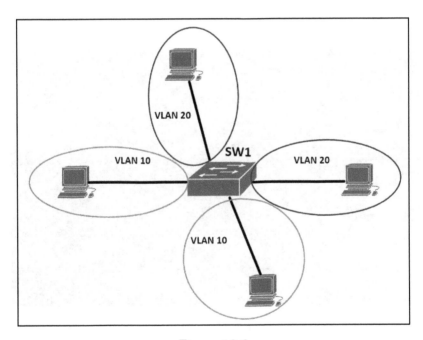

Figure 12.2

The Benefits of VLANs:

Since we are talking about VLANs, here are a few of the benefits these are bringing to networks:

1) *Security* – the separation (isolation) of networks at a logical level

2) *A better design* – separating a company into departments (each department representing a VLAN (Network))

3) *Increasing Performance* – by limiting the broadcast traffic, which is significantly bigger in large networks

4) *Scalability* – other VLANs can be easily added without impacting the network's flux

These are **represented** through an **ID** (a number between 1 and 4094).

```
SW1#show vlan

VLAN Name                             Status    Ports
---- -------------------------------- --------- -------------------------------
1    default                          active    Fa0/1, Fa0/2, Fa0/3, Fa0/4
                                                Fa0/5, Fa0/6, Fa0/7, Fa0/8
                                                Fa0/9, Fa0/10, Fa0/11, Fa0/12
                                                Fa0/13, Fa0/14, Fa0/15, Fa0/16
                                                Fa0/17, Fa0/18, Fa0/19, Fa0/20
                                                Fa0/21, Fa0/22, Fa0/23, Fa0/24
1002 fddi-default                     act/unsup
1003 token-ring-default               act/unsup
1004 fddinet-default                  act/unsup
1005 trnet-default                    act/unsup

VLAN Type  SAID    MTU   Parent RingNo BridgeNo Stp  BrdgMode Trans1 Trans2
---- ----- ------- ----- ------ ------ -------- ---- -------- ------ ------
1    enet  100001  1500  -      -      -        -    -        0      0
1002 fddi  101002  1500  -      -      -        -    -        0      0
1003 tr    101003  1500  -      -      -        -    -        0      0
1004 fdnet 101004  1500  -      -      -        ieee -        0      0
1005 trnet 101005  1500  -      -      -        ibm  -        0      0
```

Figure 12.3

As you can see in figure 12.3 from up here, on the Cisco Switches, there are a few **reserved VLAN IDs** (which can be used). These IDs are:

- **1 - VLAN-ul default**, assigned to all the interfaces of the Switch

- **1002 - 1005** – these VLANs are reserved for older technologies (FDDI, Token Ring) that practically are no longer being used nowadays

Interfaces types on a Switch

Having what I've said earlier, now you're perhaps wondering *how we can apply these VLANs* on the Switch? How are they being configured?

Before we get to the configuration part, I must mention that there are two types of special interfaces on the Switch: **Access and Trunk**. VLANs are being configured on the ports of Switches, which have to be configured in one of the previously mentioned ways.

So, the two names represent:

- **Access** – allows the passing of **ONLY one VLAN**
- **Trunk** – allows the passing of **multiple VLANs**

We configure the **Access** ports when **there is an end device** (figure 12.4) (PC, Laptop, Server, etc.)

We configure the **Trunk** ports when there is a Switch at the other end (figure 12.4) because we want to permit the passing of many VLANs through and between these.

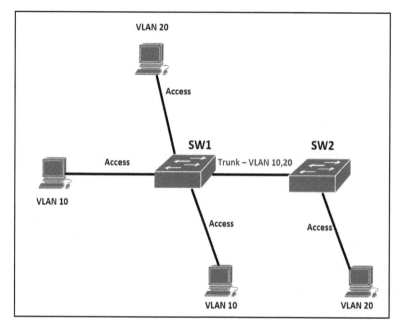

Figure 12.4

For example, if the Trunk interface between SW1 and SW2 had only VLAN 10 configured, SW2 wouldn't have been capable of sending traffic meant for VLAN 20 to the PC connected to SW2. This is why it's very important that the moment we set up a Trunk port, we verify many times if we included all the VLANs.

2.1) Configuring VLANs on Cisco Switches

Let's presume we have the following network made of 2 Switches, 4 PCs and 2 VLANs (10 and, respectively, 20):

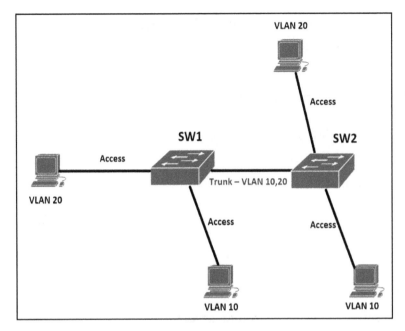

Figure 12.5

Two of these PCs are in the VLAN 10, and the other two are in the VLAN 20. To configure a VLAN on Switch, we have to follow the next steps (from the config terminal):

SW1(config)#**vlan** 10
SW1(config-vlan)#**name** IT
SW1(config)#**vlan** 20
SW1(config-vlan)#**name** HR

In this stage, we created the VLANs and assigned them a name (IT for the VLAN 10 and HR for the VLAN 20). We need to setup these VLANs on the interfaces of the devices connected to the Switch.

NOTE: these VLANs are configured on **EACH** Switch from the network (SW1 and SW2)

2.2) Configuring the Access Interface

An Access Interface permits the passing of traffic from **ONE VLAN** (in our case, 10 **or** 20) through it. This will be *configured on the connection between the Switches and the PCs* as follows:

a) We will configure the interface FastEthernet 0/1 as being Access for the VLAN 10:

SW1(config)#**interface** fa0/1
SW1(config-if)#**switchport mode access**
SW1(config-if)#**switchport access vlan** 10

b) And the FastEthernet 0/2 interface, we will set it for the VLAN 20 Access as well:

SW1(config)#**interface** fa0/2
SW1(config-if)#**switchport mode access**
SW1(config-if)#**switchport access vlan** 20

2.3) Configuring the Trunk Interface

A **Trunk Interface** allows the passing of traffic from more VLANs (in our case, 10 **and** 20). This will be *configured on the connection between Switches* in the following way:

SW1(config)#interface fa0/24

SW1(config-if)#switchport mode trunk

SW1(config-if)#switchport trunk allowed vlan 10,20

Until now, we have configured the two network equipment, the VLANs 10 and 20, we've set up the ports at which the computers are connected in the Access mode, we've added each PC in its VLAN, and in the end, we've configured the interface between the Switch as being Trunk.

Now, the PCs from the same VLAN (10 – 10) **will be able to communicate**, and the ones in different VLANs **won't be able to communicate** (10 – 20).

WARNING: these configurations must be applied on the other Switches, too, in this case, also on the SW2.

2.4) Settings Verification

After so much configuring, the time has come to verify what we have set up on our Switches. Of course, the #1 Element that we care about is connectivity. But connectivity between which end-devices? Between them all? Well, no. Why? Because we have end devices in 2 different VLANs, these can't communicate between them (only the devices belonging to the same VLAN).

So, we will ping for the equipment in VLAN 10 and then for the equipment in the VLAN 20, and in the end (to prove what we have said earlier), we'll ping between 2 devices in different VLANs (with a specific IP address for each PC in the network).

Verification for VLAN 10:

>ping 192.168.10.10

Verification for VLAN 20:

>ping 192.168.20.20

Verification for VLAN 10 - 20:

>ping 192.168.10.10

3) Routing Between VLANs

This section will talk about how we can do the **routing between VLANs**. By default, the **Switches don't know how to work with IP packages** (only with MAC addresses), which means they **won't** be able to make data transfer (routing) from a VLAN to another. This is why we need the Routing process between VLANs. This can be made in 3 ways:

A) Using a Router with as many interfaces as how many VLANs exist (this model is not a scalable one because, on the Routers, we have a limited number of interfaces)

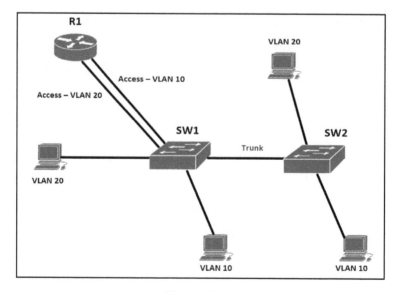

Figure 12.9

This is probably the less efficient way to make the routing between VLANs possible. Why? Because we need as many interfaces on the Router as VLANs exist (which is 99% of the cases is not possible because the Router, by design, has a low number of interfaces 3 – 5). So, this method doesn't scale and we need other options.

B) Using a Router connected to a Switch with only one interface

(Trunk) through which we will allow the passing of more VLANs – this model is known as **Router-on-a-Stick (RoaS)**

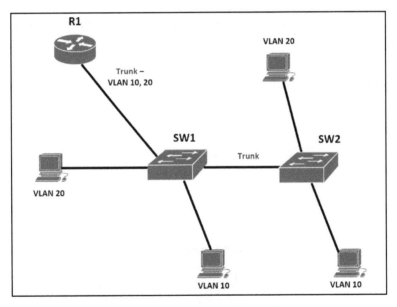

Figure 12.10

As we said earlier, this routing mode of traffic between VLANs is called Routing on a Stick (RoaS), and it will be the subject of our discussion. This way of making routing possible is old-fashioned but pretty much employed in networks. From my own experience, I can tell you that even big corporations are using this method because it's easy to implement, and the costs are greatly reduced.

The **Router-on-a Stick** concept is very simple. It allows the passing of more VLANs through a single interface (Trunk), which is connected between the Router and the Switch. On the Switch, the interface will be configured as Trunk, and on the Router, subinterfaces for each VLAN will be created.

However, it has to be taken proper care of at the charging level of the network band (bandwidth) because, after all, two or more VLANs are using THE SAME interface to communicate between them. In this case, it advised that the Router's interfaces be of at least 1 Gbps.

C) Using a Level 3 Switch (L3) – capable of making the routing (to send packages between VLANs)

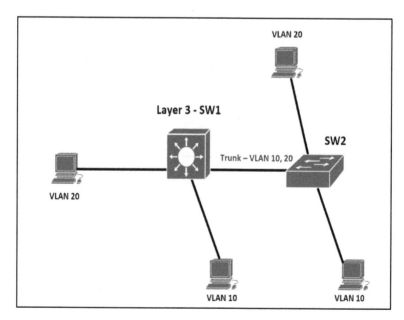

Figure 12.11

This way to make the routing between VLANs possible is, by far, the most rapid and efficient. Why? Because we have in the middle a Switch Layer 3, which can easily make the routing between VLANs possible. The advantage of using this type of Switch is that it can offer us much higher speeds (in the local network) as the routing is between Hardware and not in the Software (like Routers are doing it). Layer 3 Switches can be a very good alternative to make the routing between VLANs possible, but we must keep in mind that they are costly.

We'll discuss this subject in the next book. :)

Configuring Routing between VLANs (Router-on-a-Stick)

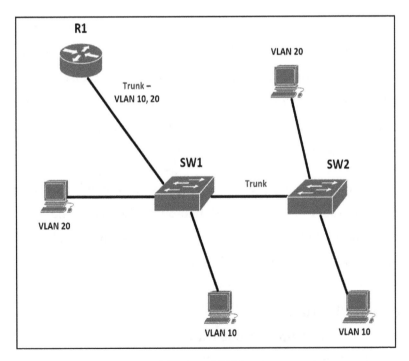

Figure 12.12

* Scenario:

Let's take the scenario from up here. We assume that recently we have created a company called RoaS, and this company develops very fast. At first, we were organized in only one department, but with the growth happening fast, this design is no longer scalable and secure, so we've decided to split the company into *departments* (IT and Sales for now).

These departments will have their own addressing space (/24) with the IPs 192.168.10.0/24 - IT and 192.168.20.0/24 - Sales.

Our purpose is for these two departments to be able to communicate with each other. Implicitly, they can't communicate with one another because a level 3 equipment (Level 3 Router or Switch) is required.

Another factor that our company needs to consider is the **cost** of the equipment. For now, we only have the budget for a Router because a Level 3 Switch is much more expensive. So, besides costs, we are also limited by the number of available interfaces on the router (usually 2-3). We have the only solution to configure the Routing between VLANs with Router-on-a-Stick.

To configure Router-on-a-Stick, we need to setup the link that connects the Switch to the Router as being Trunk; on the Router, we need to turn on the physical interface and configure the same number of subinterfaces (ex: Fa0/0.10) as the number of VLANs:

SW1(config)#**interface** Fa0/24
SW1(config-if)#**switchport mode trunk**
SW1(config-if)#**switchport trunk allowed vlan** 10,20
R1(config)#**interface** Fa0/0

R1(config-if)#**no shutdown**

Now is the moment to configure the subinterfaces for each VLAN. In the upper scenario, we have 2 VLANs, 10 and 20. To configure these subinterfaces for each VLAN, we need to follow the subsequent steps:

R1(config)#**interface** Fa0/0**.10**

R1(config-if)#**encapsulation dot1q** 10

R1(config-if)#**ip address** 192.168.10.1 255.255.255.0

R1(config)#**interface** Fa0/0**.20**

R1(config-if)#**encapsulation dot1q** 20

R1(config-if)#**ip address** 192.168.20.1 255.255.255.0

By applying these commands on the Router, communication between networks will be possible.

LAB #6

Now I came to the laboratory part (the practical part), which you in-cluded in the attachments. Here we are going to implement the ones dis-cussed above. Follow your existing lab requirements and configure the existing devices accordingly.

SCOP: Applying the Switching concepts (VLANs, Trunks and RoaS)

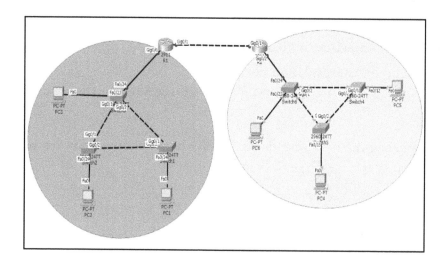

TIP: Use this commands guide (http://amzn.to/2pkG0Oq) **to solve the exercise successfully!**

You can download the labs from the following link. Click here (http://bit.ly/IT-Labs)

Chapter 13

Network Services (DHCP, ACL, NAT)

In the next section, we will talk about some network services (DHCP and NAT) and away we can protect our network. We will use as a reference the topology below:

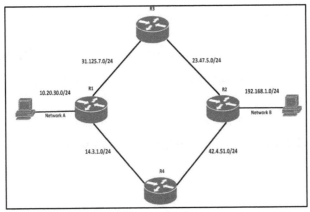

Figure 13.1

1) DHCP

DHCP (Dynamic Host Configuration Protocol) is a network protocol that dynamically provides us with the following information:

1. *IP address + Mask*
2. *Default Gateway*
3. *DNS Server*

The IP address and network mask will help us identify each device in the network (IP) and establish network size (network mask). The DNS server helps us translate the name (ex: google.com) into an IP address (216.58.214.227)

All this information is provided by a server (in smaller networks, that's what the Router does).

How does DHCP work?

When a device (PC, smartphone, tablet, Smart TV, etc.) connects to the network, it will send a Broadcast request (to all devices in the network), hoping to find a server to allocate an IP address:

1) DHCP Discover

When a DHCP server (in small networks will generally be a Wi-Fi Router) sees such a message in the network, it will immediately respond with a:

2) DHCP Offer (containing the information listed above)

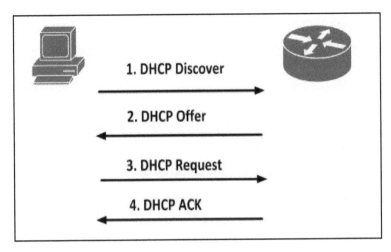

Figure 13.2

Finally, the device (PC in this case) will agree to the DHCP server's "offer" and will send a request for it:

3) DHCP Request

After receiving this message, the DHCP server responds with a

4) DHCP ACK // in confirmation of the request received from the device (PC)

Configure DHCP on the Router

To configure a Router as a DHCP Server, consider the following:

1. Network Address and Mask - (10.20.30.0/24)
2. IP Address of the gateway (router) - (10.20.30.1)
3. DNS server IP address - (8.8.8.8)

Each of these three elements is essential to ensure connectivity to the Internet at any end device (PC, phone, server, etc.). Here's how we can set them up:

R1(config)#ip dhcp excluded-address IP_1 IP_2

R1(config)#ip dhcp pool NUME

R1(config-dhcp)#network 10.20.30.0/24

R1(config-dhcp)#default-router 10.20.30.1

R1(config-dhcp)#dns-server 8.8.8.8

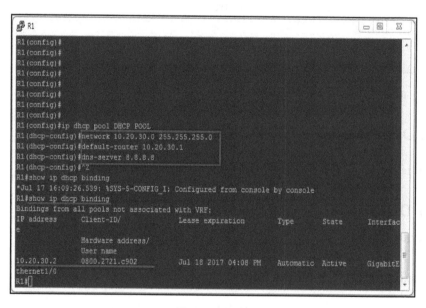

Figure 13.3

Here are some verification commands:

R1#show ip dhcp binding

R1#show run | dhcp

Configure dynamic IP address (via DHCP) on Windows

We'll take another example and see how we can allocate an IP address via DHCP on Windows XP / 7 / 8.1 / 10. We'll see how we can do this for both the CMD and Graphics.

1. DHCP from CMD

The way we can allocate an IP address through DHCP in Windows, from CMD, is through the command:

>ipconfig /renew

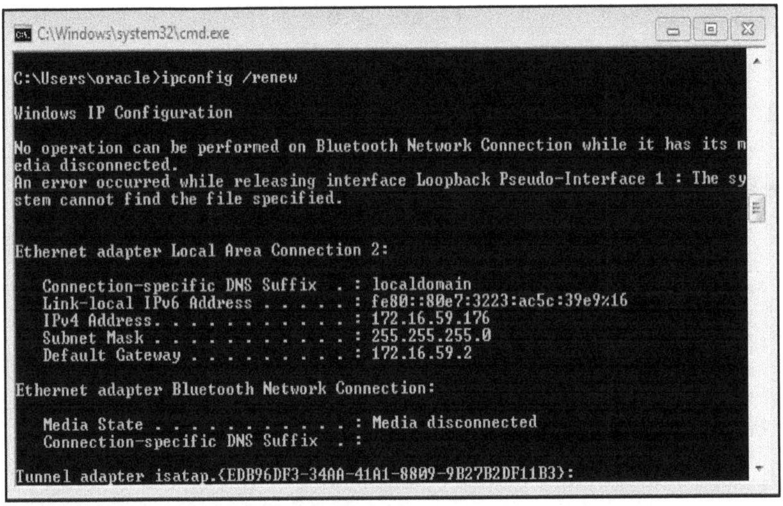

Figure 13.5

The outcome? O IP address, mask and default gateway. If we want to find more information (such as DNS, MAC address, or even DHCP server), we have the command:

>ipconfig /all

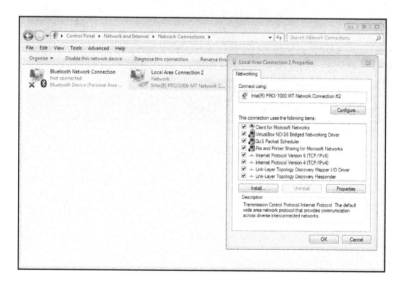

Figure 13.6

2. DHCP through the GUI

Once at this point, we can set up an IP address:

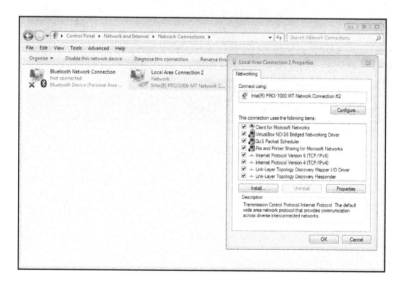

Figure 13.7

We will select IPv4 -> "Properties" and get to the window in the figure below:

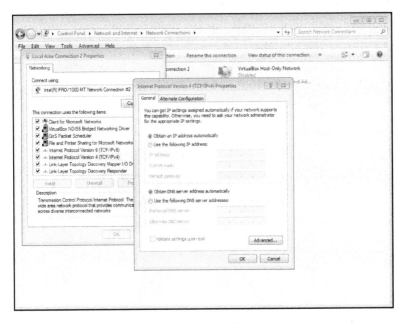

Figure 13.8

Here we can see the "Obtain an IP address automatically" and "Obtain DNS server address automatically" options. These two options will tell the PC to send a DHCP request to the network for a dynamic IP address.

LAB #7

Now I came to the laboratory part (the practical part), which you included in the attachments. Here we are going to implement the ones discussed above. Follow your existing lab requirements and configure the existing devices accordingly.

PURPOSE: Configure DHCP in LANs and recap the routing protocols.

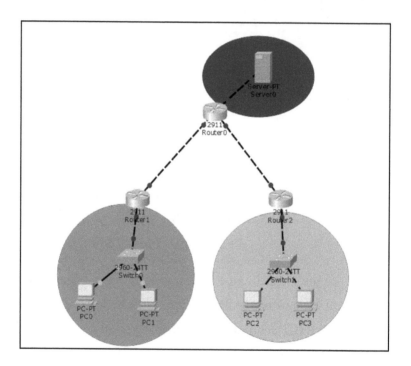

TIP: Use **this commands guide** (http://amzn.to/2pkG0Oq) to solve the exercise successfully!

You can download the labs from the following link. Click here (**http://bit.ly/IT-Labs**)

2) ACL

An Access Control List (ACL) is a set of rules to block or allow access from a network to a specific resource. These rules are set to Routers or Firewalls.

ACLs are the basis of the security concept (access limitation) in one or a network (e.g., From the Internet to the LAN - or vice versa).

Think of this concept as a Bodyguard sitting at the entrance of a club where a private party is organized. He will have a list of all the guests at that party. As people try to get in, the bodyguard will check each one; he will look on the list (ACL) and decide for each person whether they are allowed in the club or not. If you are on the list, you will be allowed to enter the party, and if you're not, your access will be denied.

We need to create these rules and include them in the ACL, for starters. As we will see below, these rules may vary: from allowing an entire network to access another network to allowing or disallowing a single PC to a server on a particular port (e.g.. SSH-22, Web-80).

After creating such an access list and adding permission or denying rules, we need to put it into operation. Specifically, we have to choose a Router (or Firewall) interface to set the direction (IN / OUT) in which we want to do this filtering.

There are two main types of ACLs:

- **ACL Standard**
- **ACL Extended**

a) ACL Standard

The purpose of Standard ACLs is to filter traffic to the source IP

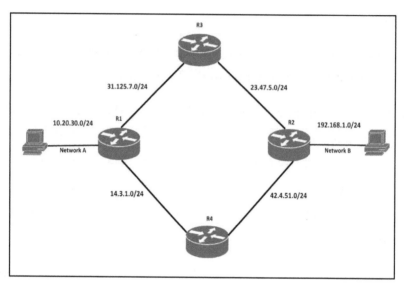

Figure 13.9

Let's say (for security reasons) the PC in Network A, with IP 10.20.30.8, and we will not be allowed to leave the LAN. So all we have to do is create an access list specifying this. The rules of this list will look like this:

R2#**deny host** 10.20.30.8
R2#**permit any**

This rule will be set to R2 on the closest server interface (in this case, the one directly connected to the server) in the OUT direction.

```
R2(config)#
R2(config)#ip access-list standard ACL_STD
R2(config-std-nacl)#deny host 10.20.30.2
R2(config-std-nacl)#permit any
R2(config-std-nacl)#exit
R2(config)#
R2(config)#interface Gi2/0
R2(config-if)#ip access-group ACL_STD in
R2(config-if)#
```

Figure 13.10

I added the 2nd line (#permit any) because, by default, at the end of each ACL, there is a "default deny" rule (#deny any). We want to stop just traffic from your PC to any other destination and allow any other traffic otherwise.

And here's the result (in the figure below) following testing on multiple devices, including your PC (you can see that 20 packets that came from it were blocked). Check using the command:

#show ip access-list

```
R2(config)#
R2(config)#do show ip access-list
Standard IP access list ACL_STD
    10 deny   10.20.30.2 (20 matches)
    20 permit any (38 matches)
R2(config)#
```

Figure 13.11

b) ACL Extended

The purpose of Extended ACLs is to filter traffic by:

- IP Source
- IP Destination
- Port Source
- Port Destination
- Protocol (IP, TCP, UDP, etc.)

Thus, this type of list gives us much greater flexibility regarding controlling. We can control any traffic flow regardless of the source, destination, and application used.

The syntax for Standard ACLs:
R#**ip access-list standard** Name

R#**permit** ip_source wildcard_mask

The syntax for Extended ACLs:
R#ip access-list extended Name

R#permit protocol ip_source wildcard_mask port_source ip_destination wildcard_mask port_destination

Setting ACLs on Interfaces

Cisco recommends the following:

- Standard ACLs are configured as close to their destination as possible

- Extended ACLs are configured as close to the source as possible

R#interface Gig 0/1

R#**ip access-group** NAME_ACL **[in/out]**

Other examples (ACL Standard):

- #deny 192.168.99.0 0.0.0.255
  - o   //will deny the whole range /24
- #permit 85.1.245.5 0.0.0.0
  - o   //will only allow this IP
- #deny 172.16.0.0 0.0.127.255
  - o   //will deny the 172.16.0.0/17 network

Other examples (ACL Extended):

- #permit ip 172.30.0.0 0.0.0.255 any
  - o   //allows traffic from source 172.30.0/24 to any destination
- #permit tcp host 10.45.21.5 eq 22 any
  - o   //allows any SSH return traffic from 10.45.21.5
- #deny udp 172.16.0.0 0.0.0.255 85.98.2.0 0.0.254.255 eq 53
  - o   //blocks DNS traffic (UDP port 53) from network 172.16.0.0/24 to 85.98.2.0/23

LAB #8

In this laboratory, we will configure the basic connectivity between Routers, after which we can proceed to the implementation of ACLs (both Standard and Extended). I invite you to follow the existing requirements in the laboratory and configure them accordingly to the existing devices.

PURPOSE: Filtering network traffic based on a set of rules. Set up ACLs.

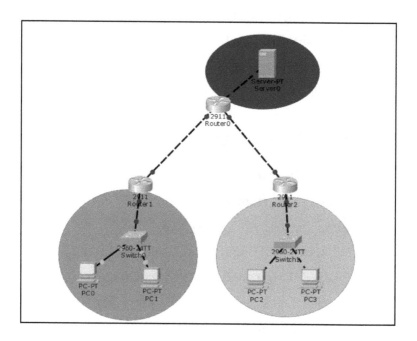

TIP: Use **this commands guide** to solve the exercise successfully!

You can download the labs from the following link. Click here (**http://bit.ly/IT-Labs**)

3) NAT

How does NAT work?

Organizations that manage the Internet (IANA) have proposed by convention that IP Private addresses can not be routed to the Internet (any package with IP source Private will be thrown!).

Thus, all ISPs have implemented traffic filtering (ACL) policies based on the IP source that verifies whether a packet has an IP private or not. If the IP source is private (i.e., 10 ..., 172.16 ... or 192.168 ...), it will be stopped and "discarded", and its transport to the destination is not allowed.

HERE intervenes NAT: Network Address Translation (NAT) masks ("translates") a Private IP into an IP Public.

Virtually without this mechanism, we could not access the internet. NAT is the Router (whether it's your company's or the one you're working on, or it's the Wireless Router in our living room)

Types of NAT

There are several types of NAT, among which we identify:

- **NAT Static**
- **NAT Dynamic**
- **PAT (Port Address Translation)**

1) NAT Static

Used for 1-to-1 mapping of a Private IP address in a Public IP address.

PC2: 192.168.1.5 -> 42.4.51.8

It is usually used when we have a server (Web, FTP, etc.) in the local area network (LAN), and we want the resources on that server (the Web page, the CS Server, a file, etc.) to either accessible from the Internet.

Example: You created a folder with pictures of the last vacation you want to share with your friends and family. You've been thinking of turning to a web server and because you have an IP Public Address and your Internet Service Provider, you've decided to turn to NAT Static.

The IP address of your server is 192.168.1.5, and the public IP is 93.1.8.6. Make the settings on your Home Router (from the Web Browser) and send your friends and family the link http://93.1.8.6/pictures_holiday2016 and they will be able to see your pictures successfully :)

2) Dynamic NAT

It makes an M-to-n mapping of a Private IP in an IP Public where m is not necessarily equal to n.

PC1: **192.168.1.6 -> 23.47.5.7**
PC2: **192.168.1.7 -> 23.47.5.8**
PC3: **192.168.1.8 -> 23.47.5.9**

Dynamic NAT uses an address space (ex: 93.1.8.7 to 93.1.8.10) which it can allocate to a single computer that wants to access the Internet. It works on the FIFO principle (first come, first served), so if we have 20 PCs in the network and only four public IP addresses available, only 4 of the 20 PCs will be able to reach the Internet.

3) PAT (Port Address Translation)

For PAT, mapping is n-to-1. We have several private IP addresses and "transform" into a single IP Public Address to which we add the Connection Source Port.

PC1: **192.168.1.6:224**13 -> 23.47.5.5:22413
PC2: **192.168.1.7:62459** -> **23.47.5.5:62459**

PAT hides multiple devices (with Private IP) behind a single Public IP. A connection between 2 devices on the Internet also includes the following items:

- IP Source
- IP Destination
- Port Source
- Port Destination

When it comes to PAT, the Router will use the IP address (Private) and Source Port to identify the connection (just as illustrated in the example above).

PAT is the most widely used NAT and is configured on most Home-Oriented Routers (TP-Link, D-Link, Asus, Huawei, Cisco, etc.).

Configure NAT on Routers

Now that we know what NAT is, how it works and how many types it is, I propose to go to the configuration side on Routers:

a. NAT Static

Static NAT is a simple mapping between a private IP address and a public IP address:

R2(config)#**ip nat inside source static** 192.168.1.2 42.4.51.9

In the end, we have to start the NAT on the interfaces:

R2(config)#**interface** Gi0/1
R2(config-if)#**ip nat inside**

R2(config)#**interface** Gi0/2
R2(config-if)#**ip nat outside**

```
R2#
R2#conf t
Enter configuration commands, one per line.  End with CNTL/Z.
R2(config)#ip nat inside source static 192.168.1.2 42.4.51.9
R2(config)#interface Gi3/0
R2(config-if)#ip nat outside
R2(config-if)#interface Fa0/0
R2(config-if)#ip nat inside
R2(config-if)#exit
R2(config)#do show ip nat translation
Pro Inside global      Inside local     Outside local     Outside global
--- 42.4.51.9          192.168.1.2      ---               ---
R2(config)#
```

Figure 13.12

As you can see in both figures, the verification command shows us the "mapping" we've done. In the figure below, we ping (from our host on Ubuntu) to a PC that is bound to R2.

It can be seen the source IP (10.20.30.2 - Ubuntu) and the public destination IP (42.4.51.9 - the PC) that are being translated into the private IP 192.168.1.2.

R2#show ip nat translation

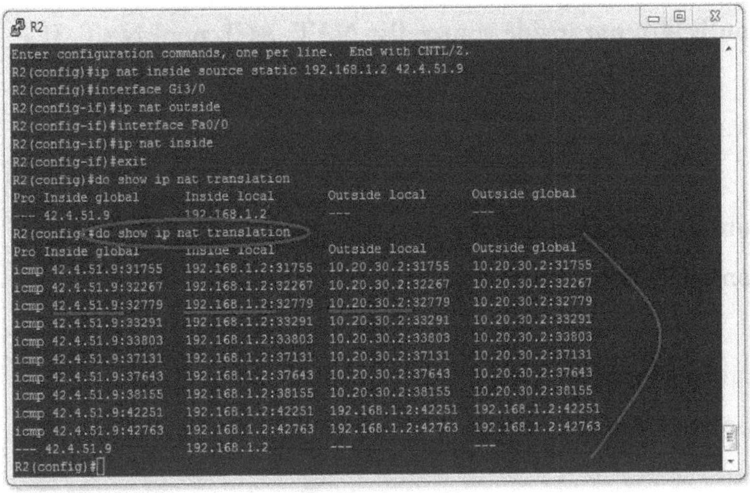

Figure 13.13

b) NAT Dynamic

To configure Dynamic NAT, we need to create a list (ACL) that identifies the IP addresses that are meant to be "NATed":

R1(config)#ip access-list standard NAT_ACL
R1(config-acl)#permit 10.20.30.0 0.0.0.255

After that, we have to set up a pool of (public) addresses that we want to allocate:

R1(config)#ip nat pool 31.125.7.11 31.125.7.14 netmask 255.255.255.0

In the end, we will create the rule that specifies the ACL and pool created earlier:

R1(config)#ip nat inside source list NAT_ACL pool NAT_IPs

And we start rules on interfaces:

R1(config)#interface Gi0/1
R1(config-if)#ip nat inside

R1(config)#interface Gi0/2
R1(config-if)#ip nat outside

```
R1(config)#
R1(config)#ip access-list standard NAT_ACL
R1(config-std-nacl)#permit 10.20.30.0 0.0.0.255
R1(config-std-nacl)#exit
R1(config)#
R1(config)#ip nat pool NAT_IP 31.125.7.11 31.125.7.14 netmask 255.255.255.0
R1(config)#
R1(config)#ip nat inside source list NAT_ACL pool NAT_IP
R1(config)#
R1(config)#interface Gi1/0
R1(config-if)#ip nat outside
R1(config-if)#
R1(config-if)#interface Fa0/0
R1(config-if)#ip nat inside
R1(config-if)#
```

Figure 13.14

Following the show order, we will see (in this scenario) a PC using a single IP address:

R1#show ip nat translation

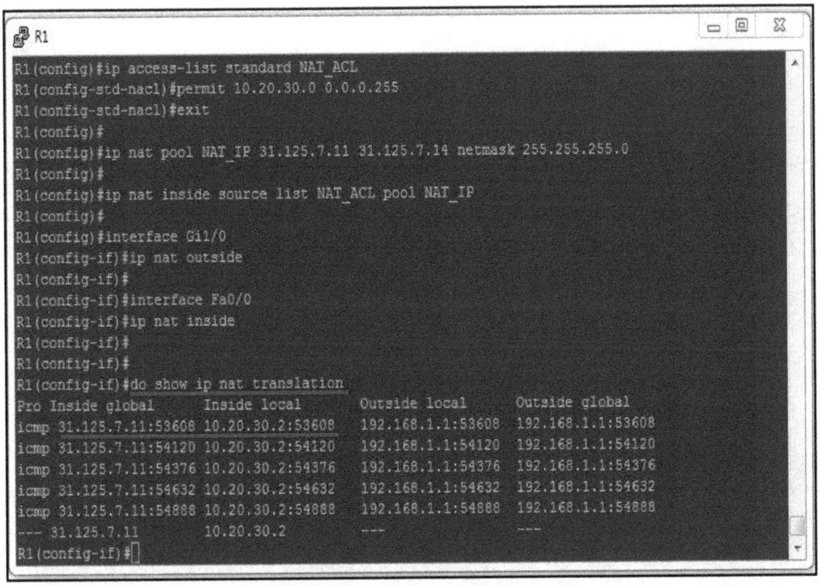

Figure 13.15

c) Port Address Translation (PAT)

To configure Dynamic NAT, we need to create a list (ACL) that identifies the IP addresses that are meant to be "NATed":

R1(config)#ip access-list standard NAT_ACL
R1(config-acl)#permit 192.168.1.0 0.0.0.255

In the end, we will create the rule by specifying the ACL and the interface we want to make the PAT, followed by the overload keyword (which says it uses the same IP address repeatedly):

R1(config)#ip nat inside source list NAT_ACL interface Gi0/2 overload

And we start rules on interfaces:

R1(config)#interface Gi0/1
R1(config-if)#ip nat inside

R1(config)#interface Gi0/2
R1(config-if)#ip nat outside

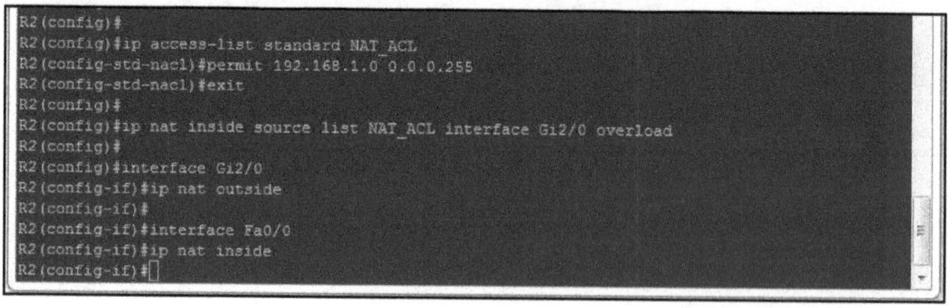

```
R2(config)#
R2(config)#ip access-list standard NAT_ACL
R2(config-std-nacl)#permit 192.168.1.0 0.0.0.255
R2(config-std-nacl)#exit
R2(config)#
R2(config)#ip nat inside source list NAT_ACL interface Gi2/0 overload
R2(config)#
R2(config)#interface Gi2/0
R2(config-if)#ip nat outside
R2(config-if)#
R2(config-if)#interface Fa0/0
R2(config-if)#ip nat inside
R2(config-if)#
```

Figure 13.16

R1#show ip nat translation

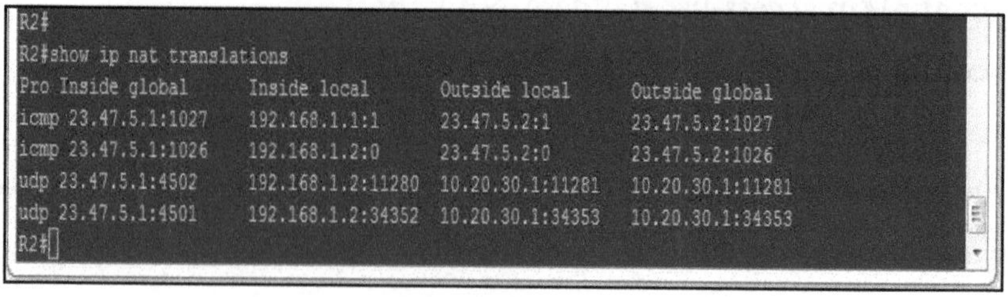

```
R2#
R2#show ip nat translations
Pro Inside global      Inside local        Outside local       Outside global
icmp 23.47.5.1:1027    192.168.1.1:1       23.47.5.2:1         23.47.5.2:1027
icmp 23.47.5.1:1026    192.168.1.2:0       23.47.5.2:0         23.47.5.2:1026
udp 23.47.5.1:4502     192.168.1.2:11280   10.20.30.1:11281    10.20.30.1:11281
udp 23.47.5.1:4501     192.168.1.2:34352   10.20.30.1:34353    10.20.30.1:34353
R2#
```

Figure 13.17

LAB #9

The lab is similar to the previous one (from ACLs), but we will configure NAT on existing network routers this time. I invite you to follow the existing requirements in the laboratory and configure them accordingly to the existing devices.

PURPOSE: Applying NAT concepts in an environment that simulates the Internet.

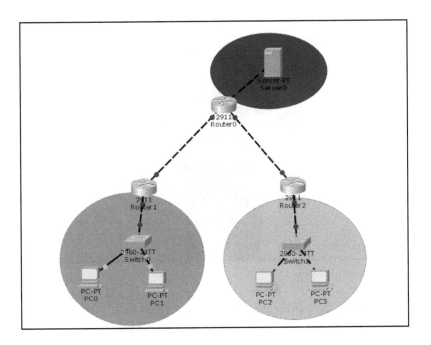

TIP: Use **this commands guide** (http://amzn.to/2pkG0Oq) to solve the exercise successfully!

You can download the labs from the following link. Click here (**http://bit.ly/IT-Labs**)

Enjoyed the book? Leave a review!

I would like to thank you for completing this book and reaching the end of it (the majority of people don't get this far). If you received value from this book, I'd like to ask you for a favour. Would you be kind enough to leave a positive review? Thank you!

You can also check out one of my other books on Amazon.com by clicking this link: https://amzn.to/2zE72Wm

Wishing you the best of luck!
Ramon Nastase
IT, Education and Optimism

PS: don't forget to claim your FREE gift here: https://bit.ly/IT-GIFT

Lightning Source UK Ltd.
Milton Keynes UK
UKHW022055130223
416920UK00013B/2177